Lynn F. Pearson

D0011225

Discovering
Famous
Graves

Shire Publications

British Library Cataloguing in Publication Data: Pearson, Lynn F. Discovering famous graves. – (Discovering; 288). 1. Sepulchral monuments – Guidebooks. 2. Tombs – Guidebooks. 3. Celebrities – Great Britain – Death 4. Celebrities – Great Britain – Tombs. I. Title. 726.8. ISBN 0 7478 0371 4

Front cover: *(Clockwise from top left) The monument marking the grave of William Hogarth, the painter, in St Nicholas's churchyard, Chiswick, London. The tomb of the local heroine Grace Darling at Bamburgh, Northumberland. The bust of the actress 'Lillie' Langtry, mistress of the future Edward VII, marking her grave in St Saviour's churchyard, Jersey. The grave of Roy Plomley, original presenter of 'Desert Island Discs', in Putney Vale Cemetery, London.*

Back cover: *A view of the memorials in section BS at Putney Vale Cemetery.*

ACKNOWLEDGEMENTS
The author wishes to thank Trevor Ermel of Monochrome, Tony Herbert and Kathryn Huggins, Caroline and Richard Pizey, Pam and Robert Hardy, Biddy Macfarlane, Sue Hudson, Jim and Margaret Perry, Anna Flowers, John Russell Lloyd, Gwyn Evans, Michael Burrell and especially John Rotheroe for their assistance in the preparation of this book.
The publishers acknowledge the kind encouragement and assistance of John Clarke, Chairman of the Brookwood Cemetery Society; John M. Humpage of the Friends of Kensal Green Cemetery; Mr and Mrs J. A. Pateman of the Friends of Highgate Cemetery; and staff at cemeteries throughout Britain who have been unfailingly helpful.
The photographs on the top right of the front cover and on pages 13, 15, 16, 21, 22, 23, 31, 49, 72, 74, 86, 87, 90 (lower), 93, 94, 118, 119, 121, 122, 123 and 131 are by the author; the remainder are by Cadbury Lamb.

Published in 1998 by Shire Publications Ltd, Cromwell House, Church Street, Princes Risborough, Buckinghamshire HP27 9AA, UK. (Website: www.shirebooks.co.uk)
Copyright © 1998 by Lynn F. Pearson. First published 1998. Number 288 in the Discovering series. ISBN 0 7478 0371 4.
Lynn F. Pearson is hereby identified as the author of this work in accordance with Section 77 of the Copyright, Designs and Patents Act, 1988.

Printed in Great Britain by CIT Printing Services, Press Buildings, Merlins Bridge, Haverfordwest, Pembrokeshire SA61 1XF.

Contents

Introduction

Before the Reformation in the sixteenth century, disposal of dead bodies was solely by church burial — under the floor of the church, for the better off, or in the churchyard, for the rest. The Reformation, with its assumption of universal membership of the established church in England and Wales, eventually forced dissenters to seek alternative burial grounds, the first of which, Bunhill Fields in the City of London, was in use by 1665. Many such burial grounds were established in provincial towns and cities during the eighteenth century.

As well as the objections of dissenters, Anglicans also began to protest at the inadequacy of urban church and churchyard burial as early as the second half of the seventeenth century. Vaults were packed with lead coffins, while churchyards were overflowing with graves, but despite this there was little improvement during the eighteenth century in England. However, in Scotland kirk burials had been halted at the end of the sixteenth century, by allowing the construction of mausolea adjoining the kirk, and Calton Hill in Edinburgh became the site of Britain's first urban cemetery in the early 1770s. It took the example of the spacious, landscaped Père Lachaise cemetery in Paris, opened in 1804, to transform the English cemetery movement into a campaign during the 1820s.

The first English cemetery, The Rosary, was established in Norwich in 1819. Here, burial was available to anyone who could pay for the service, irrespective of denomination. But it was in London and the industrial cities of northern England where the cemetery movement was most successful, with the opening of such famous cemeteries as St James, Liverpool, in 1829 and Kensal Green, London, in 1833. After these came a wave of splendid urban cemeteries, adorned with high-quality monumental architecture, including chapels and mausolea. Many of the mid-nineteenth-century cemeteries were established as private enterprises by cemetery companies. In order to cater for poorer members of the public, the Burial Acts

An early engraving of Kensal Green cemetery.

of 1852-7 set up local burial boards throughout the country, which had a duty to provide burial grounds where interment would be cheap and decent.

The practice of cremation began to find favour towards the end of the nineteenth century; the Cremation Society was founded by Sir Henry Thompson, the Queen's surgeon, in 1874. The Society built a crematorium at St John's, near Woking, and the first official cremation took place in 1885. Glasgow, Manchester and Liverpool built crematoria in the 1890s, followed by London in 1902. Around seventy per cent of funerals now involve cremation rather than burial.

Many Victorian and Edwardian urban cemeteries suffered years of neglect and mismanagement during the mid twentieth century, but changing attitudes to architecture and urban planning during the 1970s resulted in a resurgence of interest. Subsequently, ecological management schemes, conservation of the structures and improved maintenance have allowed many urban cemeteries to combine their original function with that of park and nature reserve.

Modern attitudes to death, burial and cremation are changing radically as traditional religion and religious rites become less important to many people. In addition, local burial is now unavailable in some areas because of the shortage of space in cemeteries; this has led to the suggestion of re-using graves, after a suitable interval. However, the funeral industry is now much more diverse: burial in 'green' cemeteries, eco-friendly funerals featuring cardboard coffins, alternative funerals including coffin transport by historic steam train and even burial at sea are all becoming more widely available as new rituals are developed to take the place of older formality.

There is still a huge depth of interest in the graves of Victorian cemeteries and country churchyards, for reasons relating to their importance in genealogical research and their place in Britain's architectural heritage. But alternatives to traditional funerals are proving increasingly popular (and therefore profitable); from one woodland burial site in 1993, the number had grown to fifty-eight in 1997. There are supermarket-style funeral parlours and even an award for 'Best Funeral Shop'. Who knows whether this plethora of alternative ends will result in happier endings?

Glossary of terms

Body stone: a massive horizontal slab of stone placed over a grave, with rounded cross-section and tapered ends; a deterrent against body snatchers.

Casket: a coffin; generally an American usage.

Catacomb: a subterranean burial place, generally having galleries with recesses for individual tombs.

Catafalque: a temporary, often wooden structure representing a tomb, and used in funeral ceremonies and processions.

Cemetery: generally, a burial ground; specifically, one offering burial to anyone able to pay for it, irrespective of denomination.

Cenotaph: an empty tomb, or a monument erected in honour of someone who is buried elsewhere.

Chest tomb: a tomb in the form of a stone or brick box, rectangular in plan and longer than it is high; also known as a table tomb. Originally designed to raise the ledger (*q.v.*) above encroaching vegetation.

Churchyard: a burial ground beside a church.

Cinerarium: a place of deposition for the ashes of the dead after cremation.

Cinerary urn: an urn used for preservation of the ashes of a cremated body.

Coffin: the box in which a corpse is enclosed for burial.

Coffin table: a raised stone block beneath the lychgate (*q.v.*), on which the coffin was rested.

Coffin tomb: a tomb in the shape of a coffin.

A coffin table under the lychgate of Pembury Old Church, Kent.

Columbarium: a subterranean structure whose walls contain numerous niches, each taking a cinerary urn (*q.v.*).

Cremation: the disposal of a corpse by incineration rather than burial.

Crypt: an underground chamber beneath the main floor of a church, often used as a burial place.

Embalmment: the preservation of a dead body using aromatic drugs to prevent decay.

Entomb: to place in a tomb, or bury.

Epitaph: words on a gravestone describing or commenting on the deceased.

Exhumation: the removal of a body from beneath the ground.

Footstone: a small stone which marked the foot of a grave, usually inscribed with initials corresponding to those of the headstone.

Garden of remembrance: a memorial garden, usually for ashes from cremations.

Grave: a pit dug out for burial of the dead; also now generally any place of burial.

Graveboard: a low rail, usually wooden, supported by two upright posts.

Gravestone: a stone placed at the head or foot of a grave or above it.

Graveyard: a burial ground.

Headstone: a stone which marked the head of a grave, often with decorative carvings and inscriptions.

Inhumation: the process of burying a body in the ground.

Interment: burial.

Frederick Leyland's railed tomb at West Brompton Cemetery, London, was designed by Burne-Jones. Leyland (1831-92), a ship-owner, was a patron of the Pre-Raphaelites.

Kerb: an edging stone around a grave.

Lawn cemetery: a cemetery laid out with informal paths crossing spacious grassland, featuring small grave markers and graves flush with the grass surface.

Ledger: a heavy horizontal stone slab placed over a grave; a deterrent against body snatchers.

Lychgate: a covered gate at the entrance to a churchyard.

Mausoleum: a magnificent, monumental tomb.

Mortuary chest: a small casket containing bones or other remains.

Mummification: embalming or otherwise preserving a dead body, especially as practised by the ancient Egyptians when preparing a body for burial.

Necropolis: a cemetery, especially an urban cemetery with many monuments.

Pedestal tomb: a chest tomb whose height is greater than its length.

Railed tomb: a grave bounded by railings, usually of iron.

Sarcophagus: a stone coffin, especially one decorated with carvings.

Sepulchre: a structure, often within a church, prepared as a burial place; now generally any burial place.

Table tomb: a chest tomb (*q.v.*).

Tomb: a small chamber, at least partly in the ground, used as a place of burial; now more generally any burial place.

Tombstone: originally a horizontal stone covering the grave, but now any type of memorial stone at a grave.

Vault: an underground chamber, usually with an arched roof, often used as a burial place.

A gazetteer of famous graves - England

BEDFORDSHIRE

CAMPTON

The poet **Robert Bloomfield** (1766-1823), author of *The Farmer's Boy* (1800), is buried here at All Saints; his grave is close to the east window of the north aisle of the church. Following illness in London, Bloomfield moved to Shefford, Bedfordshire, in 1814. He died there in great poverty in 1823, leaving a widow and four children, and was buried at nearby Campton, it being Shefford's mother church.

CARDINGTON

Cardington was the home of the Whitbread family of brewers. In the family vault at St Mary's church lie brewer **Samuel Whitbread** (1720-96) and his son, the politician **Samuel Whitbread** (1764-1815). The elder Whitbread was apprenticed to a London brewer in 1736, eventually running his own business and by the 1780s becoming the largest London brewer. The younger Whitbread ran the brewery for three years following the death of his father, after which it was turned into a large partnership (although he retained a majority shareholding). He committed suicide in 1815, apparently feeling his public life was at an end. In the north transept of St Mary are monuments to both men; that of the younger, dating from 1849, shows Whitbread and his wife both kneeling.

In the churchyard extension, north-west of the church and across the road, is the tomb of the victims of the R101 disaster. The airship crashed in France on its maiden voyage in 1930, killing forty-nine passengers, including **Lord Thomson of Cardington** (1875-1930), the Minister for Air. The large table tomb by the entrance gate was designed by Albert Richardson.

BERKSHIRE

BASILDON

The agricultural writer **Jethro Tull** (1674-1741), who was born at Basildon, moved to Prosperous Farm, near Hungerford, around 1709. He died there and was buried at the church of St Bartholomew in Basildon. A memorial stone was placed on the outside of the south wall of the nave in 1960.

COOKHAM

The grave of the artist **Sir Stanley Spencer** (1891-1959) may be found by entering the churchyard of Holy Trinity from Churchgate (south of the church) and taking the gravel path that bears left past the tower. Just to the left of the path, about halfway to the tower, are the Spencer family graves, with the small white headstone of Sir Stanley to the fore. Sir Stanley Spencer was born in Cookham and spent most of his life there; many of his paintings depicted the village as the background for biblical scenes.

READING

Henry I (1068-1135), king of England, died at Angers in Normandy and was buried in the chancel of Reading Abbey, which is now in ruins, in 1136. A stone indicates the approximate spot.

SLOUGH

The astronomer **Sir William Herschel** (1738-1822) is buried in the church of St Laurence, Upton Court Road, Upton. Herschel was appointed court astronomer in 1782 and in the same year moved from Bath to a large dilapidated house in Datchet, just east of Windsor. In 1785 he exchanged this house for another in Windsor and finally moved to Slough in 1786. His house there, where telescopes were set up in the garden, became known as The Herschels, and Slough became a place of scientific pilgrimage. Herschel's grave lies inside the church, beneath the tower; the gravestone is protected by a carpet. On the north wall is a stone memorial tablet bearing an inscription that includes the words '*Coelorum percipit claustra*' ('He breaks through the barriers of the heavens').

SUNNINGDALE

The film actress **Diana Dors** (1931-84), born Diana Mary Fluck, is buried in Sunningdale Cemetery, off Station Road, beside her third husband, actor **Alan Lake** (1940-84). Dors, always a popular actress, was much admired for her courageous battle against cancer; Lake never got over his grief at her death and committed suicide on 10th October 1984, the sixteenth anniversary of their first meeting. Their matching white marble headstones are carved with daffodils.

SWALLOWFIELD

The novelist **Mary Russell Mitford** (1787-1855) is buried in All Saints' church-yard, where a tall, plain stone cross, erected by public subscription north-east of the church, marks her grave. The extravagant lifestyle of Mitford's father forced her to attempt to earn a living by writing. In order to economise, she and her parents moved in 1820 from their large house near Reading to the village of Three Mile Cross, just to the south. Then in 1851 she moved a few miles further south to Swallowfield, where she lived until her death. *Our Village* (1824-32) describes rural life in the area of Three Mile Cross and also mentions Swallowfield church.

WINDSOR

Within the precinct of Windsor Castle is St George's Chapel, where a slab in the second bay of the chancel, on the south side, marks the site of the tomb of **Henry VI** (1421-71). He was originally buried at Chertsey Abbey; the tomb was taken to Windsor in 1484, but removed during the Reformation. **Edward IV** (1442-83) is buried between the high altar and the north aisle. In a vault beneath the centre of the chancel lie **Henry VIII** (1491-1547), his third wife, **Jane Seymour** (1509?-37), and **Charles I** (1600-49). The tomb of **Edward VII** (1841-1910) is on the south side of

The body of Charles I was carried into St George's Chapel, Windsor, in a snowstorm under the watchful eyes of Parliamentary soldiers.

The Royal Mausoleum in Windsor Home Park was built by Queen Victoria in 1868 as her memorial to Prince Albert. The designer of the domed Italianate structure was Ludwig Gruner, while the marble carving of Victoria and Albert, which lies directly under the dome, was carried out by Carlo Marochetti. The interior of the mausoleum is beautifully decorative, with many religious murals and its starry blue dome. The mausoleum is open to the public each year for just three days in May.

the high altar, while the bodies of **George V** (1865-1936) and his queen consort, **Mary** (1867-1953), lie in a large tomb in the second bay of the north side of the nave. The tomb of **George VI** (1895-1952) stands in a side chapel adjoining the north aisle of the choir. **Philippa of Hainault** (1314?-69), queen of Edward III, was also buried in St George's Chapel, in a tomb built by her husband and sited on its south side.

In the Royal Vault beneath the nearby Albert Memorial Chapel are **George III** (1738-1820), **George IV** (1762-1830) and **William IV** (1765-1837).

The Royal Mausoleum, Frogmore, built during 1862-71 in Windsor Home Park, contains the bodies of **Queen Victoria** (1819-1901) and her husband **Prince Albert** (1819-61).

To the rear of the Royal Mausoleum at Frogmore is a quiet lawn, well screened by shrubbery, which serves as the burial ground for many minor figures from the Royal Family. In 1957, when **Edward VIII, Duke of Windsor** (1894-1972), and Mrs Wallis Simpson, **Duchess of Windsor** (1896-1986), were contemplating their eventual burial, they bought a plot at the Green Mount Cemetery in Baltimore, USA. The Duke had already ruled out burial in St George's Chapel, as his wife would never be allowed to join him there. However, a few years later the Queen let it be known that the Duchess would be welcomed at Frogmore. So in 1972 the Duke was buried on the lawn at Frogmore, near the garden in which he played as a child. His grave, under a plane tree, is marked by a simple slab of cream Portland marble. The Duchess joined him there in 1986.

YATTENDON

The architect **Alfred Waterhouse** (1830-1905) lived in Yattendon for many years, building his home, Yattendon Court or 'The House on the Hill', from 1878 (it was demolished in 1926). He was lord of the manor and built a reading room, well house (now bus shelter) and school in the village. He died at Yattendon and was buried in the churchyard of St Peter and St Paul. His grave is marked by the tallest cross behind the church, and there is a memorial to him on the north wall of the nave. Also commemorated on the north wall, in a Latin inscription, is the poet **Robert Seymour Bridges** (1844-1930), appointed Poet Laureate in 1913. He and his mother moved to the Manor House at Yattendon in 1882. Two years later Bridges married Monica Waterhouse, the daughter of his neighbour Alfred Waterhouse. In 1905 the couple went abroad for the sake of Monica's health, returning in 1907 to settle near Oxford. A third wall memorial is to **Edward Mauger, first Baron Iliffe** (1877-1960), the newspaper proprietor, who is buried north of the church, beyond Waterhouse.

BUCKINGHAMSHIRE

AMERSHAM

Ruth Ellis (1926-55) was the last woman to be hanged in Britain. Her crime was the murder of her lover, the racing driver David Blakely, at a Hampstead pub on Easter Sunday 1955. She was originally buried in the precincts of Holloway Prison, London, but around 1970, when part of the prison was demolished, her remains

were reburied in the churchyard of St Mary, Church Street, Old Amersham. Ellis's grave is no longer marked, as most headstones have been cleared from the churchyard.

BEACONSFIELD

In the churchyard of St Mary and All Saints, the grave of the poet and orator **Edmund Waller** (1606-87) is signalled by a pyramidal obelisk mounted on a tomb-chest situated just south-east of the chancel. Waller's family seat was at Gregories, half a mile (nearly a kilometre) north-west of the church; the house was the centre

The tomb of the poet Edmund Waller (1606-87) at the church of St Mary and All Saints, Beaconsfield, is marked by a massive obelisk and is the largest in the churchyard. As well as a badly worn Latin inscription, it bears the words of Waller's fellow poet John Dryden: 'Among the poets of the age he was acknowledged to be the best.'

The eighteenth-century Octagon Temple (now a chapel) in the grounds of Cliveden is the burial place of Nancy and Waldorf Astor. The temple, which stands on a beautiful site overlooking the Thames, was designed around 1735 by the Italian country-house architect Giacomo Leoni for the Earl of Orkney. Cliveden is a National Trust property sometimes open to the public, although the house is now an hotel.

of a vast estate. Waller, banished from England in 1644 on account of his plot to seize London for Charles I, was pardoned in 1651 and returned from France to build Hall Barn, an elegant house just south of Beaconsfield. Gregories and its estate was bought in 1768 by the statesman and political theorist **Edmund Burke** (1729-97), whose grave is inside the church; it is marked by a brass plate under the seventh pew from the front on the south side of the nave.

In the Catholic cemetery on the north side of Shepherds Lane stands the tombstone of the writer **Gilbert Keith Chesterton** (1874-1936) and his wife Frances (d.1939). (Shepherds Lane leads off from the White Hart roundabout in Old Beaconsfield.) The stone, which is on the path leading east from the back of the chapel, bears reliefs of Christ Crucified and the Virgin by Eric Gill, dating from 1937 and 1939. Chesterton lived in Beaconsfield from 1909 until his death. His home was Overroads, the first house to be built on Grove Road, itself the first of the new suburban streets cut through the Gregories estate. Top Meadow, opposite Overroads, was built for Chesterton in 1912 as his studio and study and was gradually enlarged in the years following.

CHALFONT ST GILES

In the churchyard of St Giles, the tomb with a standing cross, beside the war memorial, is that of **Bertram Wagstaff Mills** (1873-1938), circus proprietor. Mills's father, a coachbuilder, owned two small farms where he sent horses to rest. Mills spent much of his childhood at one of these farms, in Chalfont St Giles, where he learnt to ride; he entered the circus business after the First World War. He died at Chalfont St Giles, his last wish being that the circus should be carried on by his two sons, which it was.

CLIVEDEN

Nancy Witcher Astor (1879-1964), Viscountess Astor, who became the first woman member of Parliament in 1919, is buried at Cliveden, the country house bought by the American-born millionaire **William Waldorf Astor**, Viscount Astor, in the 1890s. Nancy married his son **Waldorf Astor** (later second Viscount Astor) in 1906. The first Viscount Astor (1848-1919) was buried in the Octagon Temple, which stands just to the south-west of the house, overlooking the Thames, and which he converted into a chapel during 1893-7; a bronze floor slab marks his grave. The second Viscount Astor was also buried in the Temple, and Nancy's ashes were eventually placed there, in her husband's grave.

GERRARDS CROSS

The actress **Dame Margaret Rutherford** (1892-1972) is buried on the north side of the island site in the extension to St James's churchyard. The words 'A Blithe Spirit' on her brown marble headstone refer to Noël Coward's *Blithe Spirit* (1941), in which she played the spiritualist Madame Arcati.

GREAT HAMPDEN

The politician **John Hampden** (1594-1643), who came from an old Buckinghamshire family, took an active part on the Parliamentarian side during the Civil War. He was mortally wounded during a skirmish with Prince Rupert at Chalgrove

The Disraeli family tomb at St Michael's church, Hughenden, near High Wycombe. Benjamin Disraeli (1804-81), twice prime minister, died in London but was buried close to his home, Hughenden Manor; there is also a monument in Westminster Abbey. As well as a politician, Disraeli was a successful novelist; he hoped to influence public opinion through his writings, declaring that 'My works are my life'.

Field, about 10 miles (16 km) west of High Wycombe, on 18th June 1643. He died at Thame and was buried at Great Hampden (near his home, Hampden House) in the church of St Mary Magdalene. His monument, put up in 1743, includes a sarcophagus and a battle scene.

GREAT MISSENDEN

Several members of the Dahl family had made their home in the Aylesbury area before the author **Roald Dahl** (1916-90) moved to Gipsy House, a farmhouse on the edge of Great Missenden, in 1954. His daughter Olivia, who died in 1962 aged seven, is buried at the nearby village of Little Missenden. Her large plot, on which Dahl built an alpine garden, was also intended for Dahl and his first wife, Patricia Neal; however, the couple were divorced in 1983. Instead, Dahl (who said that he could not fully believe in Christianity) was buried on the hillside opposite Gipsy House, in the churchyard of St Peter and St Paul, Church Lane, Great Missenden. His grave is just above that of his step-daughter, who had died a few months earlier. They are marked by plaques in the lawn cemetery, a few metres below a small tree.

HUGHENDEN

In the churchyard of St Michael is the grave of the novelist and politician **Benjamin Disraeli** (1804-81), MP for Buckinghamshire from 1847 to 1876, created first Earl of Beaconsfield in 1876, and prime minister during 1868 and 1874-80. The tomb has blue railings and is adjacent to the east wall of the chancel; a marble memorial to Disraeli, erected by Queen Victoria, may be found inside the chancel. The church stands on a hillside just below Hughenden Manor, which was bought by Disraeli in 1847 and much altered by him in 1862-3. Disraeli's father lived at Bradenham Manor, about 3 miles (5 km) west of Hughenden.

JORDANS

The Quaker and founder of Pennsylvania **William Penn** (1644-1718) is buried at the Friends' meeting house. Penn was granted land in America by Charles II in payment of a debt to his father, Admiral Sir William Penn, in 1682. He drew up the constitution for the new colony, which he named Pennsylvania, living there during 1682-4 and 1699-1701. His last home was at Ruscombe, near Reading. Quaker

In front of the Friends' meeting house at Jordans is a peaceful burial ground, where the small headstone marking the grave of the Quaker leader William Penn (1644-1718) may be found amongst other Penn family graves (at the left of the front row). The clarity and simplicity of the headstones make an attractive and compelling contrast with the typically decorative stones found in many churchyards.

meetings had been held in the Jordans area since the mid seventeenth century, then at Old Jordan's Farm, just north of the meeting house, from at least 1669 until the meeting house itself was erected in 1688. The burial ground was bought in 1671. Penn's grave is marked by a stone at the far end of the row opposite a single stone, near to the meeting house.

LITTLE MARLOW

In the village cemetery is the grave of the novelist, playwright and journalist **(Richard Horatio) Edgar Wallace** (1875-1932); it is on the east side of the cemetery, beside the path, and is marked by a tall white stone cross. Wallace, whose home was at once-fashionable Bourne End, just east of Little Marlow, wrote over 170 novels and was best known for his thrillers. He died in Hollywood, where he was working on the screenplay for *King Kong*.

MARLOW

North-west of the tower of the parish church is the grave of the 'Penny Show-man', **John Richardson** (b.1767). Back to back with his square-topped headstone is that of George Gratton, 'the Spotted Boy', a fairground freak in Richardson's show.

John Richardson and his 'Spotted Boy' (shown here in a contemporary print) are buried together in Marlow churchyard.

OLNEY

The divine **John Newton** (1725-1807) is buried in the churchyard of St Peter and St Paul, where he had been curate. This slaver turned hymn-writer was originally buried at St Mary Woolnoth in the City of London, where he was incumbent, but his remains were translated here in 1893.

PENN

The British diplomat and Soviet spy **Donald Duart Maclean** (1913-83) is buried in the main churchyard of Holy Trinity. Maclean defected to the USSR in 1951 and died in Moscow, where he was cremated. His ashes were brought back to England by his elder son and buried in the family plot at Penn, marked by a Saxon cross on an octagonal base within a kerb, by the west boundary of the churchyard. To the right of the archway to the churchyard extension is an alcove seat commemorating **Sir Ambrose Heal** (1872-1959), founder of the eponymous London store, and his family. Within the extension, designed by Sir Edward Maufe in 1976, is the grave of **Alice Jane (Alison) Uttley** (1884-1976), children's author, who lived locally; she also published *Buckinghamshire* in 1950. Her headstone, on the right of the left-hand path, calls her 'A spinner of tales'.

SPEEN
    In the burial ground of the Baptist chapel is the grave of the typographer and stone carver (**Arthur**) **Eric (Rowton) Gill** (1882-1940) and his wife Mary Ethel Gill (1878-1961). His home from 1928 was Pigotts (Gill's spelling), a house at Piggott's Hill, Speen. Gill had converted to Roman Catholicism in 1913, and following his death a mass was held in the chapel he had built at Pigotts. Afterwards, the coffin was trundled in procession down the hill on a farm cart to the nearest acceptable burial ground, the Baptist chapel in Speen, where his grave, by the upper boundary hedge, is marked by plain, rounded head and foot stones bearing an inscription of his own design. Also in this line of graves is a later occupant of Pigotts, **Bernard Robinson** (1904-97), the founder of the Music Camp Movement.

STOKE POGES
    The massive monument – a sarcophagus on a 20 feet (6 metres) high square pedestal – just east of the churchyard of St Giles commemorates the poet **Thomas Gray** (1716-71) and his *Elegy Written in a Country Church-Yard*. Soon after the death of Gray's father in 1741, his mother and aunt moved to West End Cottage (now reconstructed as Stoke Court) in Stoke Poges. Gray often visited them and completed his *Elegy*, begun in 1742 and perhaps referring to the local churchyard, in the village in 1750; it was published the following year. The monument was built in 1799 by John Penn (grandson of William Penn, founder of Pennsylvania) of nearby Stoke Park, partly as an eyecatcher for the park. A plain brick tomb-chest in the churchyard marks Gray's grave, the northern one at the eastern end of the church.

WEST WYCOMBE
    The body of **Sir Francis Dashwood** (1708-81), Baron Le Despencer, Chancellor of the Exchequer 1762-3, lies in the Dashwood Mausoleum, stunningly situated on a hill just north of his house in West Wycombe Park. Dashwood succeeded to the estate in 1724 and, after devoting his early life to travelling and pleasure seeking, restored the church of St Lawrence (near the mausoleum), rebuilt West Wycombe House, laid out its gardens and erected the mausoleum (1764-5). Dashwood died at West Wycombe.

CAMBRIDGESHIRE

CAMBRIDGE
    The ashes of the author **Charles Percy Snow** (1905-80), Baron Snow, are kept in an urn beside the pond in the Fellows' Garden at Christ's College, St Andrew's Street. C. P. Snow, a physicist, was best known for his depiction of the two cultures, science and arts; he was a fellow of Christ's, and then a tutor there during 1935-45.
    St Giles's church stands on Castle Street but its churchyard is about half a mile (nearly a kilometre) out of town, on the south side of Huntingdon Road. (Take the narrow All Souls Lane on the left shortly after Fitzwilliam College.) The churchyard, now called Ascension Parish Burial Ground, has many distinguished academics buried in it, including two of Charles Darwin's sons. There is an excellent location panel by the chapel listing many of the better-known occupants. These include **George Edward Moore** (1873-1958), the philosopher appointed to the Order of Merit, **Sir Desmond MacCarthy** (1878-1952), the journalist and drama critic, and **Sir John Douglas Cockcroft** (1897-1967), atomic physicist and Nobel prizewinner. Cockroft, once a member of Ernest Rutherford's team at the Cavendish Laboratory in Cambridge, became Master of Churchill College, Cambridge, in 1959. (These three graves are adjacent to the drive to the chapel.) Also buried here is the social anthropologist **Sir James George Frazer** (1854-1941), author of *The Golden Bough*, a twelve-volume epic on the themes of magic, religion and science, published between 1890 and 1915. Frazer spent most of his life in Cambridge, where he was a fellow of Trinity College during 1879-1941. His grave is marked by

a plain grey marble ledger, north of the chapel. Also under a grey stone ledger, south-west of the chapel, is the philosopher **Ludwig Josef Johann Wittgenstein** (1889-1951), who studied at Trinity College, Cambridge, in 1912-13; he returned in 1929, becoming professor of philosophy during 1939-47. **Sir Denis William Brogan** (1900-74), the Scottish historical writer and broadcaster, specialised in the history of North America and originated the BBC *Transatlantic Quiz*. He is buried under a slate headstone in the north-east corner of the graveyard extension.

The exact fate of the remains of the Lord Protector **Oliver Cromwell** (1599-1658) is unclear. Cromwell, who matriculated from Sidney Sussex College, Cambridge, in 1616, was buried in the Henry VII Chapel at Westminster Abbey, but his body was disinterred and hung at Tyburn in 1661. This was followed by decapitation, the body probably ending up in a pit near the gallows (where the southern end of the Edgware Road now is), or it may have been transferred to St Nicholas's church, Chiswick. Cromwell's head, however, was mounted on a spike in front of Westminster Hall, and there it stayed for over twenty years before being blown down. The head passed through many hands until it came into the possession of Sidney Sussex College in 1960 and was buried near the entrance to the college chapel; the spot is not marked.

CHIPPENHAM
Sir Thomas Erskine May (1815-86), first Baron Farnborough, was clerk of the House of Commons in 1871-86. He wrote the *Rules, Orders and Forms of Procedure of the House of Commons* in 1854 whilst a taxing-master for both Houses of Parliament. He was buried in the churchyard of St Margaret in Chippenham, west of the south porch.

FENSTANTON
The grave of the landscape designer **Lancelot 'Capability' Brown** (1716-83) is

A detail from 'Capability' Brown's chest tomb in the church of St Peter and St Paul at Fenstanton. The monumental chest, made of Coade stone, is inscribed with a eulogistic verse by the poet and landscape gardener William Mason. In addition to Brown's tomb, a modern commemorative stone stands in the churchyard.

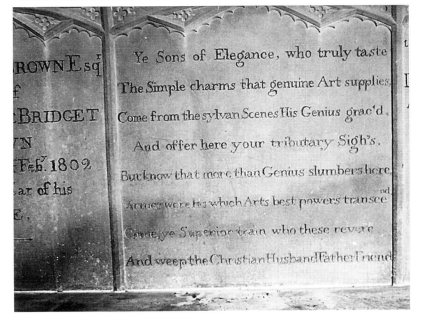

outside the north wall of the chancel of St Peter and St Paul; it is marked by a modern headstone. His monument is a tomb-chest on the inside wall of the chancel on which a verse describes Brown as possessing 'more than Genius'. Brown was head gardener at Stowe before moving to London in 1751. He bought a small estate at Hilton and Fenstanton in 1767 and acquired the manor of Fenstanton in 1770, the year in which he served as High Sheriff of Huntingdonshire.

HELPSTON
The poet of rural life **John Clare** (1793-1864), born and raised in Helpston, is buried in the churchyard of St Botolph, as he had wished. His coffin stone, inscribed 'A poet is born not made', is by the south wall of the chancel. A monument to Clare stands in the centre of the village.

PETERBOROUGH
Catherine of Aragon (1485-1536), the first wife of Henry VIII, is buried in the north choir aisle of Peterborough Cathedral. She died at Kimbolton House, north-west of St Neots.

CHESHIRE

KNUTSFORD
The novelist **Elizabeth Cleghorn Gaskell**, née Stevenson (1810-65), was brought up in Knutsford, the original of *Cranford* (1853). She attended the Brook Street Unitarian chapel and is buried in its graveyard, with her husband and two of her four daughters.

NORTHENDEN
The railway promoter **Sir Edward William Watkin** (1819-1901), first baronet, began his career in his father's cotton firm in Manchester, then became involved with railway management from 1845. He was High Sheriff of Cheshire in 1874. He died at Rose Hill, Northenden, near Cheadle, and was buried at Northenden parish church.

PORT SUNLIGHT
William Hesketh Lever (1851-1925), first Viscount Leverhulme, is buried in the graveyard of Christ Church in Port Sunlight, the village he began building from 1888 as accommodation for the factory workers who produced his 'Sunlight' soap. The graves of Lever and his wife may be found in a small enclosure adjacent to the church.

SALE
The physicist **James Prescott Joule** (1818-89), best-known for his research into the mechanical equivalent of heat, is buried at the north-east end of Brooklands Cemetery, Marsland Road. Joule, the son of a Salford man, became President of the Manchester Literary and Philosophical Society in 1860.

WARRINGTON
The comedian **George Formby** (1904-61) was born George Hoy Booth but adopted the same stage name as his father, a music-hall comedian. He went on the stage in 1921, taking up the ukulele four years later. He is buried, with his father, in the Catholic section of Warrington Cemetery, Manchester Road. Turn left at the entrance and where the drive splits into three take the central path to an open circle. The large white memorial, with a medallion portrait of Formby senior, is on the left.

CORNWALL AND THE ISLES OF SCILLY
FOWEY
The ashes of the novelist **Dame Daphne Du Maurier** (1907-89) were scattered

Above left: *This is a view through the lychgate at the church of St Enodoc, near Trebetherick, the little Cornish village where Sir John Betjeman stayed every summer when a boy. The top of the secluded, sloping churchyard provides a fine view of the Camel estuary and its sandy beaches.*

Above right: *Sir John Betjeman's black slate headstone in the churchyard at St Enodoc, one of the first churches he explored as a child.*

by her children on the cliffs near her home, Menabilly House, Fowey. Many of her books, including her most famous novel, *Rebecca* (1938), were set in the West Country, where she spent much of her life.

The prolific writer **Sir Arthur Thomas Quiller-Couch** (1863-1944), known as 'Q', was the son of a Cornish doctor. His home from 1892 until his death was The Haven, a house situated just above the Polruan Ferry in Fowey. Quiller-Couch was Mayor of Fowey in 1937-8 and set many of his novels there. He died after being hit by a car whilst out walking near his home and was buried in the churchyard of St Fimbarrus.

ISLES OF SCILLY

Harold Wilson (1916-95), Baron Wilson of Rievaulx, prime minister 1964-70 and 1974-6, had a holiday home on the Isles of Scilly for over forty years. He was buried on the islands, in the churchyard of St Mary the Virgin.

MYLOR

The journalist and novelist **(Robert) Howard Spring** (1889-1965) moved to Cornwall in 1939, buying a bungalow beside Mylor Creek. The success of his novels allowed him to retire from journalism, and in 1947 he moved to a large Georgian house in Falmouth, where he died in 1965. His ashes were laid on the north side of the churchyard of St Mylor.

ST IVES

In St Ives Old Cemetery lies the most unusual grave of the artist **Alfred Wallis** (1855-1942). Wallis, who took up painting at the age of seventy, was 'discovered' at St Ives in 1928 by Ben Nicholson and Christopher Wood. His works, mainly depicting ships, were executed with decorator's paint on scraps of board and inspired a trend towards abstract painting. Wallis's low chest tomb is topped with painted stoneware tiles designed and made by Bernard Leach; the tiles show a lighthouse amidst stormy seas and describe Wallis as 'artist & mariner'.

TREBETHERICK

The grave of the poet, architectural writer and broadcaster **Sir John Betjeman** (1906-84) is in the sheltered churchyard of St Enodoc, just south of Trebetherick. The little chapel lay buried in the sands until dug out and restored in 1863; now it stands amidst the St Enodoc golf links. As a child, Betjeman spent family summer holidays at Trebetherick; in adolescence, when church architecture became his great enthusiasm, he visited St Enodoc, which he always loved. His beautifully carved slate headstone stands just to the right of the path on entering the churchyard through the lychgate.

CUMBRIA

BRIGFLATTS

The ashes of the poet **Basil Bunting** (1900-85) were scattered in the Quaker graveyard here, near the Friends' meeting house. Bunting, who was born and lived for much of his life in Northumberland, visited the Brigflatts area when a child and

The ashes of the fellwalker and author Alfred Wainwright (1907-91) were scattered on his favourite fell, Haystacks. In his own words, 'Haystacks stands unabashed...in the midst of a circle of much loftier hills, like a shaggy terrier in the company of foxhounds...but not one of this distinguished group of mountains...can show a greater variety and a more fascinating arrangement of interesting features.'

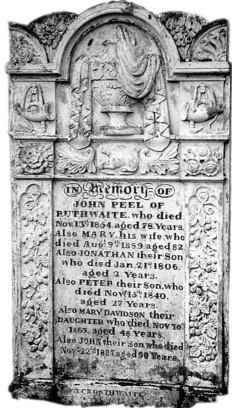

Standing stark and white in the churchyard of St Kentigern in Caldbeck is the tall headstone marking the graves of the huntsman John Peel (1776-1854) and his family. The handsome and highly decorated stone portrays two hunting horns and a hound in repose.

named his famous poem *Briggflatts* (1966) after the hamlet. It was where he felt most at home; it seemed to sum up his feelings for Northumbria.

BUTTERMERE

The ashes of the Lakeland fellwalker, guidebook writer and illustrator **Alfred Wainwright** (1907-91) were scattered beside Innominate Tarn on Haystacks, a fell to the south-east of Buttermere. There is a memorial plaque in the village church, below the most westerly window on the south side, which gives a view of the fell. The wording suggests that you 'Lift your eyes to Haystacks, his favourite place'.

CALDBECK

The Cumberland huntsman **John Peel** (1776-1854) kept a pack of hounds at his own expense in Caldbeck for fifty years. His fame arises from the song 'D'ye ken John Peel'. His grave in the churchyard of St Kentigern is marked by a tall, whitewashed headstone near the wall, just south of the west end of the church. The stone stands amongst many other Peel family graves and is decorated with two hunting horns and a watchful hound.

CHAPEL STILE

The ashes of the historian **George Macaulay Trevelyan** (1876-1962) lie in the churchyard of Holy Trinity, Great Langdale, in Chapel Stile. Trevelyan's family home was Wallington in Northumberland, a county which he loved; however, the Lake District came a close second in his affections. He often stayed with friends at Stool End in Great Langdale, about 2 miles (3 km) west of Chapel Stile; he was a tireless walker and a keen conservationist. He acquired a cottage in Langdale shortly before the First World War. Trevelyan married in 1904; his first son, Theodore, was born in 1906 but died in 1911; he is buried in the Great Langdale churchyard, just east of the church. The ashes of his parents were eventually laid there too.

CONISTON

The grave of the artist, critic and social reformer **John Ruskin** (1819-1900) may be found in the churchyard of St Andrew; it is marked by a tall cross made from Tilberthwaite stone. Ruskin stayed in Keswick as a child but bought the Brantwood estate, on Coniston Water, in 1871 and lived there from 1872 until his death.

Donald Malcolm Campbell (1921-67), who broke the world speed records on land and on water, died on Coniston Water when his boat *Bluebird* broke up during an attempt to break his own water speed record; his body was never recovered.

GRASMERE

In the black-railed Wordsworth family enclosure at the south-east corner of St Oswald's churchyard, by the river Rothay, are the graves of the poet **William Wordsworth** (1770-1850) and his sister, the writer **Dorothy Wordsworth** (1771-1855). The headstone marking the grave of William and his wife Mary is in the centre of the front row, while Dorothy's headstone is two to the left. William Wordsworth was born and raised in Cumbria. After a long separation, in 1794 he and Dorothy spent some weeks at a farmhouse owned by friends just north of Keswick, before moving first to Dorset and then to Somerset, near the home of Samuel Taylor Coleridge, a fellow poet and hill-walker whom Wordsworth had met in 1795. In 1799 William and Dorothy settled at Dove Cottage, Town End, Grasmere (Coleridge was a guest during 1800), but moved to Allan Bank, a larger house just north-west of the town in 1808, when Dove Cottage became too small for their needs. In 1811 they moved to the old vicarage and two years later to Rydal Mount, south-east of Grasmere, where William died in 1850. After many years of illness, Dorothy died in 1855.

The grave of **William Archibald Spooner** (1844-1930) can be found in Grasmere town cemetery, on Pye Lane. Entering the cemetery via the gate nearest the village, follow the path as it curves gently left, and the grave is on the right, the third headstone across on the third row down. Spooner, Warden of New College, Oxford, was famous for his 'Spoonerisms', in which the initial letters of two words were transposed. He and his wife had enjoyed holidays in Grasmere for many years, staying at his wife's house, How Foot.

GREAT CROSTHWAITE

Robert Southey (1774-1843), one of the Lake Poets, met Samuel Taylor Coleridge while a student at Oxford in 1794. Coleridge stayed with William and Dorothy Wordsworth at Town End, Grasmere, in 1800 and eventually rented Greta Hall, on the hills west of Keswick, as a family home. In 1802 Southey visited Coleridge, and, after Coleridge moved away because of ill-health in 1803, Southey took over Greta Hall, where he remained until his death in 1843. He is buried in the churchyard of St Kentigern in the village of Great Crosthwaite, about a mile (1.5 km) north-west of Keswick. Restoration of his grave has been funded by the Brazilian government in memory of his *History of Brazil* (1810-19). A monument may be found inside the church; it is a recumbent white marble figure, showing Southey with one hand on his heart and the other holding a book.

Robert Southey

KESWICK

Sir Hugh Walpole (1884-1941), artist and author of the Herries novels, which are set in Lakeland, lived at Brackenburn near Grange in Borrowdale. Some of his manuscripts and paintings are at Keswick Museum and Art Gallery, and he is buried in the churchyard of St John's.

The grave of the author Arthur Ransome and his second wife, Evgenia Shelepin (1894-1975), once Trotsky's secretary, in the churchyard at Rusland. Ransome went to Russia in 1913 and remained to cover the revolution as a reporter for the 'Daily News'. He met Evgenia there and they married in 1924.

NEAR SAWREY

The ashes of **Helen Beatrix Potter** (1866-1943), the writer and illustrator of children's books, were scattered in a field on her farm at Near Sawrey; the exact site is unknown. Potter and her parents, with whom she lived in London, stayed at Near Sawrey during the summer of 1896, and she thought it to be a perfect place. Her book *The Tale of Peter Rabbit* was published in 1901, its royalties enabling her to buy Hill Top Farm, Near Sawrey, in 1905. Her visits to Hill Top became ever longer, and she eventually moved there; it featured in several of her later books. After her marriage to William Heelis in 1913, and a move across the road to Castle Cottage, Potter concentrated on farming matters and the National Trust.

RUSLAND

The author **Arthur Michell Ransome** (1884-1967) spent holidays near Coniston Water as a child and lived in the southern Lakes for much of his life. His interest in country pursuits is reflected in his series of children's books, which were often set in the Lake District, beginning with *Swallows and Amazons* (1930). After a spell in Russia, Ransome lived at Low Ludderburn, a farmhouse set high above the south-eastern end of Lake Windermere, during 1925-35. He was lord of the manor of Lowick, just south of Coniston Water, during 1947-9, when he lived at Lowick Hall. Finally he moved to Hill Top, Haverthwaite (just south of Lake Windermere), in 1963. From his home there were splendid views along the Rusland valley; later, exploring this area, Ransome discovered the quiet and isolated Rusland churchyard. He decided he wished to be buried there and now lies, with his second wife, in a corner of the little churchyard of St Paul, deep in the remote Furness Fells, south-west of Lake Windermere.

DERBYSHIRE

AULT HUCKNALL

Thomas Hobbes (1588-1679), the philosopher and author of *The Leviathan* (1651), is buried in the church of St John the Baptist. Hobbes, a protégé of the Cavendishes, was tutor to two Earls of Devonshire. He spent the last years of his life at Hardwick Hall, just south of Ault Hucknall, and died at Hardwick in 1679. Inside the church, his monument is a black slab on the floor of the south aisle, beneath its east window.

CHESTERFIELD

George Stephenson (1781-1848), the inventor and railway entrepreneur, took a lease on Tapton House, a large brick house on the north-eastern edge of Chesterfield, around 1840 while working on railway construction in the area. Stephenson died in Chesterfield and is buried beneath the communion table of Trinity church, Newbold Road. The stained glass of the east window is his memorial.

CROMFORD

The engineer and inventor **Sir Richard Arkwright** (1732-92) built the first successful water-powered cotton-spinning mill in Cromford in 1771. He was a pioneer in the industrialisation of cotton manufacturing, building not only several highly efficient mills but an entire village for his workforce at Cromford. He bought the manor of Cromford in 1789 and had begun building a country house, Willersley Castle, near the village when he died. His grave lies in the church of St Mary, Mill Road, Cromford, which he began building in 1792; it was completed in 1797.

DERBY

Elizabeth Talbot (1518-1608), Countess of Shrewsbury, known as 'Bess of Hardwick', was a formidable builder of great houses, including Hardwick Hall. She died at Hardwick 'in a hard frost while her builders could not work'. She was buried in the Cavendish family vault beneath the south chancel chapel of what is now the Cathedral Church of All Saints in Derby; it was raised to cathedral status in 1927. Over forty members of the Cavendish family were buried beneath the chapel between 1607 and 1848; a wall monument with her recumbent effigy commemorates Bess of Hardwick.

EDENSOR

Sir Joseph Paxton (1801-65), gardener, architect and designer of the Great Exhibition building (the Crystal Palace) in 1851, planned the new village of Edensor for his employer, the sixth Duke of Devonshire. After his death at Sydenham, his body was brought back to be buried in the centre of the churchyard of St Peter.

The massive sculptured head of Sir Joseph Paxton dominates the grounds of Crystal Palace at Sydenham in South London.

KEDLESTON

George Nathaniel Curzon (1859-1925), first Marquess Curzon of Kedleston, Conservative politician and Viceroy of India, is buried in All Saints' church, which stands in the grounds of Kedleston Hall, the Curzon family home since the twelfth century.

DEVON

DARTMOUTH

The novelist **Flora Jane Thompson** (1876-1947) had worked as a clerk in the Post Office before marrying John Thompson, who became a postmaster. They moved to Dartmouth in 1928, where her husband ran the post office while her writing progressed from journalism to books. *Lark Rise*, the first part of an autobiographical trilogy, was begun in 1937 and published in 1939. After her husband's retirement in 1940, they moved to Brixham. She is buried in Long Cross Cemetery, Dartmouth.

GEORGEHAM

The author and journalist **Henry Williamson** (1895-1977) is buried in the churchyard of St George; his headstone bears his personal owl symbol. He moved to Georgeham, on the edge of Exmoor near Bideford Bay, in 1921 after being deeply affected by his experience as an army officer during the First World War. He took a small cottage and lived a simple country life, inspired by the writings of Richard

A splendidly carved owl looks out from the headstone of the author Henry Williamson in the churchyard of St George, set just above the little village of Georgeham. His home there from 1947, Ox's Cross, was a hut that he built himself of elm planks on an oak frame. The owl was Williamson's personal symbol.

Jefferies, and published *Tarka the Otter* in 1927. In 1930 he left to farm in Norfolk, but, after a short spell of internment because of his pro-Hitler views, he returned to Georgeham in 1947. His home, until his death in 1977, was a hilltop hut he had built himself.

LEW TRENCHARD
The antiquarian **Sabine Baring-Gould** (1834-1924), composer of the hymn 'Onward Christian Soldiers', inherited the family estate at Lew Trenchard in 1872, moving to Lew Manor with his own family in 1881. With the aid of local craftsmen, he transformed this simple home into a neo-Jacobean manor house. He was squire of Lew Trenchard during 1877-1924 and rector in 1881-1924; the church of St Peter, also much altered by Baring-Gould, is in a valley near Lew Manor. Baring-Gould is buried in the churchyard, his grave marked by a plain headstone.

SHEEPSTOR
A large sarcophagus of red Aberdeen granite marks the grave of **Sir James Brooke** (1803-68) at St Leonard's church. He was the first Rajah of Sarawak and bought the local Burrator estate in 1858.

SHIRWELL
Sir Francis Charles Chichester (1901-72), airman, sailor and navigator, was the younger son of the vicar of Shirwell and was born in the village. He won the first single-handed transatlantic yacht race in 1960 and was knighted by the Queen in 1967 after his solo circumnavigation of the world. He was taken ill during the fourth transatlantic race in 1972 and died shortly afterwards in Plymouth. He is buried in the churchyard of St Peter, Shirwell.

DORSET
BOURNEMOUTH
In the churchyard of St Peter, Hinton Road, a splendid white marble sarcophagus, to the right at the top of the steps from the south door of the church, signals the grave of **Mary Wollstonecraft Shelley** (1797-1851), author of *Frankenstein, or the Modern Prometheus* (1818). She died in London but was buried in Bournemouth, near Boscombe Manor, the home of her son. She was buried with the heart of her husband, the poet **Percy Bysshe Shelley** (1792-1822), whose ashes lie in the

Protestant cemetery, Rome. Also sharing the grave are Mary Shelley's son, his wife and Mary's parents, the philosopher and author **William Godwin** (1756-1836) and **Mary Wollstonecraft** (1759-97), author of *A Vindication of the Rights of Women* (1792). The remains of the Godwins were brought to Bournemouth from old St Pancras churchyard, London, soon after Mary Shelley's death in 1851 by her son, as the churchyard had been partially destroyed by railway construction (although their headstones are still there).

At Wimborne Road Cemetery, Wimborne Road, Bournemouth, a large marble cross about 50 yards (45 metres) from the east side of the chapel, just left of the path, marks the grave of the statesman **Evelyn Baring** (1841-1917), first Earl of Cromer.

BROADSTONE

The collector and naturalist **Alfred Russel Wallace** (1823-1913), who with Charles Darwin published the theory of evolution in 1858, is buried in Broadstone cemetery, Gravel Hill. His grave, adorned by a petrified tree-trunk on a plinth, is halfway down the main path on the right. Wallace moved house frequently, in search of country life, taking a house at Parkstone in 1889 and finally settling nearby at Broadstone in 1902.

CHESIL BEACH

The ashes of the author **John Cowper Powys** (1872-1963) were scattered on the sea at Chesil Beach, near Abbotsbury. He was brought up in the Dorset and Somerset countryside, which provided the background for many of his novels.

LYME REGIS

The grave of the geologist **Mary Anning** (1799-1847), discoverer of the first complete fossil ichthyosaurus, is in the churchyard. She was a native of Lyme Regis. A memorial window is in the church.

MORETON

The Arabic scholar and traveller **Thomas Edward Lawrence** (1888-1935), better known as 'Lawrence of Arabia', rented the cottage called Clouds Hill, 9 miles (15 km) east of Dorchester, in 1923 when he was stationed at nearby Bovington

The grave of T. E. Lawrence in the new cemetery at Moreton, a small village in the Frome valley. The complexities of Lawrence's character and his various roles as writer, man of action – 'Lawrence of Arabia' – and aircraft hand are hardly reflected in this elegant but uninspiring headstone.

Only Thomas Hardy's heart lies beneath this tombstone in the churchyard of St Michael at Stinsford; his ashes lie in Westminster Abbey. This bizarre arrangement resulted from a clash between Hardy's own wishes, to be buried at Stinsford, and those of his family, friends and admirers, who felt that an abbey funeral would be more appropriate.

Camp. He bought the cottage in 1925 as a retreat and retired to live there in 1935. He died the same year in a motorcycle accident near Clouds Hill and was buried at Moreton, just over a mile (nearly 2 km) south-west of the cottage. His grave is in the new cemetery, which is opposite the road to the church.

PORTLAND BILL

The ashes of the sex educationist **Marie Charlotte Carmichael Stopes** (1880-1958) were scattered off Portland Bill. Her country home was in the village of Easton on the Isle of Portland.

SHERBORNE

In Sherborne Abbey church lie the remains of **Ethelbald** (d.860), king of the West Saxons, and **Ethelbert** (d.866), king of Wessex.

STINSFORD

The heart of the author **Thomas Hardy** (1840-1928), man of Dorset, is buried in the churchyard of St Michael, beside his first wife; his parents are buried nearby. Stinsford featured as Mellstock in *Under the Greenwood Tree* (1872). Hardy, who sang in the choir of St Michael as a child, settled in 1885 just outside Dorchester at Max Gate, a house built to his own design. It was always Hardy's wish that he should be buried at Stinsford, but as a Westminster Abbey funeral had been planned the heart was removed from the body before cremation and brought to Stinsford, while the ashes were placed in the south transept of the abbey. The Poet Laureate **Cecil Day-Lewis** (1904-72), who wrote detective fiction using the name Nicholas Blake, is also buried in the church-

Near Thomas Hardy's grave at Stinsford is the handsome headstone of the poet Cecil Day-Lewis. He is buried here because of his great admiration for Hardy and his love of Dorset.

29

yard. He attended Sherborne School and loved the county of Dorset; his grave is close to that of Hardy, whom he admired greatly.

TOLPUDDLE
The Friendly Society of Agricultural Labourers was founded in Tolpuddle in 1834. Six members took an oath of mutual support; this crime led to them being tried, condemned and sentenced to seven years transportation to New South Wales. There was an immediate public outcry, but the 'Tolpuddle Martyrs' had already been taken out of the country; they were not pardoned until 1837. They came back to England the following year, but only one, **James Hammett** (1811-91), returned to live in Tolpuddle. His grave, with a headstone by Eric Gill, is in the village churchyard.

WIMBORNE MINSTER
The tomb of **Ethelred I** (d.871), king of Wessex, may be found in the sanctuary of Wimborne Minster; its stone slab bears a fifteenth-century brass effigy of the king.

DURHAM

DURHAM
The tomb of the **Venerable Bede** (673-735), the scholar monk, is inside the galilee of Durham Cathedral. Bede spent most of his life teaching at St Paul's monastery in Jarrow and was originally buried there. His body was moved to Durham in 1020 and transferred to the southern side of the galilee in 1370. The plain but impressively large tomb-chest has a black marble top. The shrine of **St Cuthbert** (d.687), Bishop of Lindisfarne, is also in the cathedral, behind the high altar. He retired to Inner Farne Island and eventually died in his cell; his body, which apparently remained unsullied for many years, was transferred to Durham in 1104. His coffin, now restored, is in the Chapter Library.

EBCHESTER
Inside the church of St Ebba lies the tomb of the sporting novelist **Robert Smith Surtees** (1805-64). Surtees, the creator of Jorrocks, was born in Durham and attended Durham Grammar School. He inherited his father's Hamsterley estate in 1838, after which he was able to devote his time to hunting and shooting. He became High Sheriff of Durham in 1856. He died in Brighton and was buried at Ebchester, 3 miles (5 km) west of his home, Hamsterley Hall.

HOUGHTON-LE-SPRING
Inside the church of St Michael and All Angels is the large tomb-chest of **Bernard Gilpin** (1517-83), 'Apostle of the North' and rector of Houghton-le-Spring. The sides of the chest have geometric decorations.

WHICKHAM
In the churchyard of St Mary, Church Green, is the grave of the oarsman and boatbuilder **Henry 'Harry' Clasper** (1812-70); the Tyneside rowing hero was born in nearby Dunston. On the day of his funeral, around 130,000 people lined the route of the cortege. The crowds made it impossible to proceed, and instead the body was taken along the Tyne by barge. To find his grave, take the path immediately west of the tower and head downhill for about 50 yards (just under 50 metres). The grave, to the left of the path, is marked by a splendid canopied monument in which Clasper is portrayed standing and wearing contemporary working class dress. There is a fine view of the river Tyne and its valley, now marred by the noise of a constant tide of traffic. To the rear of Clasper's monument is a standing stone shaped to resemble the prow of a rowing boat; this was erected

The sturdy sandstone figure of the oarsman Henry 'Harry' Clasper (1812-70) looks out over the river Tyne from the pretty churchyard of St Mary at Whickham, near Gateshead. The sculptor of the Clasper memorial (now listed grade II) was a local man, George Burn, whose work was popular in the 1870s.

by Clasper and his brothers in memory of their mother. Other Clasper family graves are nearby.

ESSEX

BARKING

The prison reformer **Elizabeth Fry** (1780-1845) died in Ramsgate and was buried at the Friends' burial ground, North Street, Barking; the headstone has disappeared. She became a Quaker minister at the age of twenty-nine and spent much of her life travelling the country to advance the cause of prison reform.

BARKINGSIDE

The philanthropist **Thomas John Barnardo** (1845-1905) opened his first boys' home in Stepney in 1870. It was the forerunner of 'Dr Barnardo's Homes', the first of which he founded in 1876: the Girls' Village Home at Barkingside. Barnardo died at Surbiton and was cremated at St John's Crematorium, Woking, Surrey; his public funeral took place at the Village Home in Barkingside. In 1908 a monument by George Frampton was erected over his tomb there.

BLACK NOTLEY

In the churchyard of St Peter and St Paul is the grave of the botanist **John Ray** (1627-1705), 'Father of Natural History' in Britain, who was born at Black

31

This decorative obelisk on its plinth marks the grave of the botanist John Ray at Black Notley, his birthplace. The obelisk was a favourite element in eighteenth-century funerary architecture.

Notley. The grave is marked by an obelisk, to which a plaque has been added by the John Ray Society; it stands close to the north wall of the nave.

COLCHESTER

Buried in Holy Trinity church, now a social history museum, is **John Wilbye** (1574-1638), composer of English madrigals, who lived in the town at the end of his life.

FINCHINGFIELD

The playwright **Dorothy 'Dodie' Smith** (1896-1990), who wrote plays under the name C. L. Anthony, was also the author of the book *The Hundred and One Dalmatians* (1956), which became a major Walt Disney film. She lived simply for many years at her seventeenth-century cottage, The Barretts, near Finchingfield. She was cremated nearby and her ashes 'scattered to the four winds', as she wished.

HEMPSTEAD

William Harvey (1578-1657), discoverer of the circulation of the blood, was initially buried in the Harvey family vault in the church of St Andrew. His body had been wrapped in lead, and in 1883 it was transferred by the College of Physicians to a white marble sarcophagus in the Harvey Chapel, which had been added to the church as its north transept. The remains of forty-nine members of the Harvey family are still in the vault below.

HIGH LAVER

The philosopher **John Locke** (1632-1704) is buried in a railed grave in the churchyard of All Saints against the south wall of the church; a tablet with an inscription he composed can now be found on the inner south wall of the church, having been moved from the churchyard in 1932. In 1691 Locke moved to Oates, the High Laver home of Sir Francis and Damaris, Lady Masham, and lived there until his death. Lady Masham, who wrote on religious topics, was much influenced by Locke's works.

Outside the east end of the church is the tomb chest of **Abigail, Lady Masham** (d.1734), who supplanted the Duchess of Marlborough as Queen Anne's confidante.

John Locke

ONGAR

The children's writer **Jane Taylor** (1783-1824) and her sister, Ann Gilbert, published a joint volume entitled *Rhymes for the Nursery* in 1806; it included Jane's most famous poem, 'Twinkle, twinkle little star'. The Taylor family moved from Colchester to Castle House, Ongar, in 1811. Three years later, following Ann's marriage, the family moved to Peaked Farm in Ongar. Jane Taylor and her parents were buried beneath the floor of the Congregational chapel, now the United Reformed church, reached through an archway in a row of cottages at the south end of Ongar's main street.

STONDON MASSEY

The composer **William Byrd** (1538?-1623) lived at Stondon Place in Stondon Massey from around 1593, eventually buying the house after a protracted dispute over its ownership. He is buried at St Peter and St Paul in an unmarked grave.

WALTHAM ABBEY

Harold II (1020?-66), king of the English, was slain at the battle of Hastings. Reputedly, his body was buried at the coast but later transferred to Waltham Abbey, where his supposed grave is marked by a stone slab in the abbey gardens at the east end of the abbey.

Near this slab, in the gardens of Waltham Abbey, may lie the body of King Harold II, killed at the battle of Hastings in 1066, in the first year of his reign. Harold was probably the first monarch to have been crowned in Westminster Abbey and was the last of the Saxon kings.

33

GLOUCESTERSHIRE

AMBERLEY

Percival Christopher Wren (1875-1941) was born (as plain Percy Wren) in Deptford. He was educated at Oxford, where he began to call himself 'Percival Christopher', and taught in India from 1903 before publishing his first novel in 1912. P. C. Wren had his first great success with *Beau Geste* (1924), a romantic story of the French Foreign Legion, although it seems he never joined its ranks. He died at Amberley and is buried in the churchyard.

BERKELEY

The grave of the physician **Edward Jenner** (1749-1823), discoverer of vaccination, may be found at the church of St Mary. Jenner was born in Berkeley and practised there from 1773, obtaining the degree of doctor of medicine from St Andrews University in 1792. There is a plaque on the wall and a commemorative window in the chancel. In the churchyard is the table tomb of the watchmaker **Thomas Pierce** (d.1665) with its much quoted epitaph.

DAYLESFORD

At St Peter is the grave of **Warren Hastings** (1732-1818), governor-general of British India for the East India Company. Hastings, whose grandfather was rector of Daylesford, grew up at the rectory and dreamt of buying back the nearby manor house and estate which his family had been forced to sell following the Civil War. After being acquitted of corruption in an expensive and lengthy trial that ended in 1795, Hastings was compensated by the East India Company; this enabled him to purchase the family estate, and he began to restore St Peter's church in 1816. His railed grave, immediately to the east of the church (which was rebuilt in 1860), is topped by a neo-Greek urn and pedestal.

GLOUCESTER

The splendid tomb of **Edward II** (1284-1327) may be found in Gloucester Cathedral. Edward was forced to resign the throne in 1327 and was cruelly murdered while imprisoned in Berkeley Castle, about 12 miles (19 km) south-west of Gloucester. The ashes of the educationalist **Dorothea Beale** (1831-1906), founder of St Hilda's College, Oxford, and principal of Cheltenham Ladies' College from 1858 until her death, were also buried in the cathedral, in a small vault on the south side of the Lady Chapel. A bronze tablet, complete with portrait, marks the site. Beale came from a Gloucestershire family and died at Cheltenham.

SAPPERTON

The graves of the craftsmen **Ernest William Gimson** (1864-1919) and brothers **Sidney Barnsley** (1865-1926) and **Ernest Barnsley** (1863-1926) may be found at the church of St Kenelm, under heavy body stones beneath yew trees either side of the path. In 1893 Gimson and Sidney Barnsley left London to live and work at the manor house in Pinbury Park, Duntisbourne Rouse, about 3 miles (5 km) north-west of Cirencester. Ernest Barnsley and his family joined them later, and all three soon settled in the village of Sapperton, a few miles to the south.

Also buried at Sapperton, in the cemetery on the Frampton Mansell road west of the village, are the ashes of the Labour politician **Sir (Richard) Stafford Cripps** (1889-1952). After his death in Switzerland, his ashes were returned to Sapperton, near his home in the Cotswolds. His headstone is on the right of the path from the cemetery gate.

SLIMBRIDGE

The ashes of the ornithologist and artist **Sir Peter Markham Scott** (1909-89) were scattered on the Doubles at Slimbridge, home of the Wildfowl and Wetlands

Trust, where he had lived for many years. There is a commemorative bust of Sir Peter by the entrance to the Wildfowl and Wetlands Centre.

TWIGWORTH
The poet and songwriter **Ivor Gurney** (1890-1937) was born in Gloucester. Gassed in the First World War, he died in an asylum in Kent, but his body was returned to his home county for burial. His grave is to the north-west of the church, marked by a Celtic cross, close to that of the family of another composer, Herbert Howells (1892-1983), whose own ashes are in Westminster Abbey. Gurney's grave was vandalised in January 1998.

WINCHCOMBE
Catherine Parr (1512-48), sixth queen of Henry VIII, is buried at Sudeley Castle, near Winchcombe. In 1543 she was forced to marry Henry VIII, but after his death in 1547 she secretly married Sir Thomas Seymour, Baron Seymour of Sudeley. She gave birth to a daughter at Sudeley Castle in 1548 and died of a fever shortly afterwards. Her tomb dates from the nineteenth century, as the original was destroyed during the Civil War.

HAMPSHIRE

BEACON HILL
On top of Beacon Hill, near Old Burghclere, is the grave of the Egyptologist **George Edward Stanhope Molyneux Herbert** (1866-1923), fifth Earl of Carnarvon. His birthplace was the Carnarvon family seat, Highclere Castle, 2 miles (3 km) to the north. In collaboration with Howard Carter, Carnarvon discovered the tomb of Tutankhamun in 1922 but died (in Cairo) before excavation was complete. As he wished, he was buried on Beacon Hill.

BINSTED
At the far west end of the churchyard of Holy Cross, marked by a grey ledger, is the grave of **Bernard Law Montgomery** (1887-1976), first Viscount Montgomery of Alamein. Field Marshal Montgomery (who played hockey for the Army in 1913) rose to prominence during the North Africa campaign of 1942. In retirement, Montgomery lived in a converted mill on the river Wey at Islington, a mile (1.5 km) from Binsted. His banner hangs in the church.

EAST WELLOW
The grave of 'The Lady with the Lamp', the nursing reformer **Florence Nightingale** (1820-1910), stands in the churchyard of St Margaret, south of the church. She was brought up at Embley Park, a large house just over a mile (1.5 km) from East Wellow. The family grave is marked by a large stone monument that is inscribed only with her initials and dates.

EVERSLEY
The author **Charles Kingsley** (1819-75) became curate of Eversley in 1842 and rector in 1844, staying until his death in 1875. He wrote many of his books, including *The Water-Babies* (1863), in the rectory. A marble cross by the churchyard wall marks his grave at St Mary's, whose north aisle was built in 1876 as a memorial to Kingsley. There is a memorial window by Christopher Webb in the chancel.

FARNBOROUGH
The French **Empress Eugénie** (1826-1920) bought the house Farnborough Hill in 1881, with the intention of erecting a mausoleum for herself and her husband, **Napoleon III** (1808-73), in its spacious grounds. She extended the house and from

The canopied monument topped by a pinnacle in the churchyard of St Margaret at East Wellow is the Nightingale family grave; its inscription acknowledges Florence Nightingale only by her initials and dates. At first her family were strongly opposed to her career in nursing. Her achievements in the medical field were rewarded in 1907 by the award of the Order of Merit, the first time it had been bestowed upon a woman.

1886 built St Michael's Abbey and the associated mausoleum (which contains their two bodies); she lived at Farnborough until her death in 1920. Also buried there is their son **Napoleon Eugene Louis, Prince Imperial** (1856-79), who was killed serving with the British army in Zululand.

FORDINGBRIDGE

The home of the artist **Augustus Edwin John** (1878-1961) was Fryern Court in Fordingbridge. He is buried in an annexe of the Town Cemetery.

HARTLEY WINTNEY

The architect, writer and teacher **William Richard Lethaby** (1857-1931), surveyor to Westminster Abbey 1906-28, retired at the end of the First World War and moved to Hartley Wintney with his wife, Edith. They lived in Albion Cottage, a house found for them by a friend, but stayed only two years, the libraries and museums of London proving too great an attraction. Edith Lethaby died in 1927 and was buried in St Mary's churchyard at Hartley Wintney. Her epitaph, on a stone which W. R. Lethaby may have designed, reads 'She was wise and true and very kind'. Lethaby was eventually buried beneath the same stone, to which the words 'Love and Labour are All' were then added.

Also buried at St Mary's, on a raised paved area by the east perimeter, was Alan Francis Brooke (1883-1963), first **Viscount Alanbrooke,** field marshal, a soldier who made a crucial contribution to the British army's eventual success during the Second World War. He and his wife are buried beneath an impressive slab with a coloured carved relief crest.

HIGHCLIFFE

The businessman **Harry Gordon Selfridge** (1858-1947), who opened Selfridge's department store in Oxford Street, London, in 1909, is buried at St Mark, in the southern part of the graveyard, about halfway down beside the west fence. Selfridge rented the Gothic mansion Highcliffe Castle for a short time.

HURSLEY

The church of All Saints at Hursley was built in 1846-8 for **John Keble** (1792-1866), the pioneer leader of the Oxford Movement, who was vicar here from 1836 until his death in 1866. In the churchyard a large marble tombstone marks his grave, which lies near the tower of the church.

LITTLE SOMBORNE

Outside the east end of the pretty little redundant church is the grave of the aircraft designer **Sir Thomas Octave Sopwith** (1888-1987), 'Pioneer Aviator'.

LYMINGTON

In Lymington cemetery, near Pennington, lies the grave of the poet **Coventry Kersey Dighton Patmore** (1823-96), author of the *The Angel in the House* (1854-63), a sequence of poems in praise of married love. Patmore lived in Hastings during 1875-91, having enjoyed the resort when on holiday with his young family. Forced to move by a change of ownership of his Hastings home, he settled at Lymington in 1891 and stayed until his death in 1896.

MICHELDEVER

Sir Francis Baring (1740-1810), founder of the financial house of Baring Brothers & Company, is buried in the family vault at St Mary. His monument by Flaxman is on the south wall of the chancel, with other Baring memorials. The

Baring family had homes at The Grange and Stratton Court in Micheldever.

MINSTEAD

The author **Sir Arthur Conan Doyle** (1859-1930), creator of the detective Sherlock Holmes, always loved the New Forest. He practised as a doctor in Portsmouth during 1882-9 but eventually made his home at a house called Windlesham at Crowborough in East Sussex. A few years before he died he bought a country retreat at Bignell Wood, near Minstead. Initially he was buried at Windlesham, in a garden grave by the summerhouse in which he worked, but when the house was sold in 1955 his remains and those of his wife were moved to Minstead. His grave, marked by a cross beneath an oak tree at the south-east end of All Saints' church-

The grave of Sir Arthur Conan Doyle and his wife Jean in the churchyard of All Saints, Minstead. The lettering at the base of the cross describes Sir Arthur as a 'patriot, physician and man of letters'.

yard, carries the inscription 'Steel true, blade straight'.

OLD ALRESFORD
Admiral George Brydges Rodney (1719-92), first Baron Rodney, built Old Alresford House, just east of the church, around 1752. He is buried with his wife Jane in a vault at St Mary's church. A grandiose monument by Cheere is on the north wall of the nave.

OTTERBOURNE
In the churchyard of St Matthew is the flat grey marble cross commemorating **Charlotte Mary Yonge** (1823-1901), author of *The Heir of Redcliffe* and over one hundred other novels. She lived in the village and her grave is to the left of the path from the lychgate, which she gave to the church.

PORTSMOUTH
The tomb of the soldier **Sir Charles James Napier** (1782-1853) is outside the west entrance of the Royal Garrison church. On his return from India in 1851 he retired to a small property at Oaklands on the Hampshire Downs, a few miles from Portsmouth, and lived there until his death two years later.

ROMSEY
Louis Francis Albert Victor Nicholas Mountbatten (1900-79), first Earl Mountbatten of Burma and admiral of the fleet, was buried at Romsey Abbey, a mile (1.5 km) north of his home, Broadlands. Mountbatten had planned every detail of the funeral himself, even including the lunch menu for mourners on the train journey between the service at Westminster Abbey and the burial at Romsey.

SELBORNE
The naturalist **Gilbert White** (1720-93) spent most of his life at Selborne, publishing his *Natural History and Antiquities of Selborne* in 1789. He was born at the vicarage and lived at The Wakes from 1729 until his death; he became curate of the village in 1751. He was buried in St Mary's churchyard. His grave, to the north of the chancel, is marked by a plain headstone carrying only his initials and date of death.

SOUTHAMPTON
The grave of the aircraft designer **Reginald Joseph Mitchell** (1895-1937) is at South Stoneham Cemetery, Swaythling; it lies on the left, beside the main drive south of the chapel. Chief engineer and designer at the Supermarine Aviation works in Southampton during 1919-37, Mitchell designed the Spitfire fighter aircraft, famed for its performance in the Second World War.

The comedian **Alfred Hawthorn 'Benny' Hill** (1924-92) died at his home at Teddington, Middlesex, and was buried in the family plot at Hollybrook Cemetery, Southampton. A few months later the grave was vandalised and Hill's coffin lid smashed in an apparent search for jewels. From the main gate, turn left at the chapel, and the black marble coffin tomb is the first grave in the seventh row.

WEST MEON
The ashes of the Soviet spy **Guy Francis de Moncy Burgess** (1911-63), who died in Moscow, were scattered on his mother's grave at St John the Evangelist's church. His name is on the cross on the bank directly north of the tower. Also here is the grave of **Thomas Lord** (1755-1832), the sportsman who founded Lord's Cricket Ground in London. He died at West Meon, and his grave is marked by a flat stone slab on a low chest tomb on the left of the path leading from the porch.

Two of the six mortuary chests which stand on the presbytery screen in Winchester Cathedral. The chests contain royal remains, including the bones of Ethelwulf, king of the Saxons, and Canute, king of the English. Having been moved from the original minster, the remains were then disturbed during the Civil War, making precise identification impossible.

WINCHESTER

Ethelwulf (d.858), king of the West Saxons and Kentishmen, and Bishop of Winchester, was buried in the cathedral. His bones are contained in a mortuary chest

on top of the presbytery screen, along with those of **Canute** (994?-1035), king of the English, who died at Shaftesbury. **St Swithun** (d.862), Bishop of Winchester, was initially buried (at his own wish) outside the north wall of the cathedral. His body was moved inside in 971, but the shrine was destroyed by Henry VIII; it was replaced in 1962 and stands near the Lady Chapel. **William II** (c.1056-1100), king of England, called Rufus, was killed by an arrow while hunting in the New Forest and buried at the cathedral. His tomb is in front of the lectern. **Izaak Walton** (1593-1683), author of *The Compleat Angler* (1653), lived at Winchester with his son-in-law, a canon of Winchester, from 1678 until his death in 1683. He was buried in Prior Silkstede's Chapel in the south transept of the cathedral. The author and original 'bluestocking', **Mrs Elizabeth**

The memorial window to Izaak Walton, author of 'The Compleat Angler', in Prior Silkstede's Chapel at Winchester Cathedral. The window, which stands above Walton's tomb, was made by Powell & Sons of Whitefriars, London, in 1914 and depicts Walton beside the river Itchen. It was given by the anglers of England and America.

Montagu (1720-1800), née Robinson, was also buried in the cathedral. So too was the author **Jane Austen** (1775-1817); her tomb is in the north aisle of the nave. She lived in the village of Chawton, near Alton, from 1809 until moving to Winchester in 1817 in order to consult a local doctor regarding her poor health; she died a few months later.

The soldier **Archibald Percival Wavell** (1883-1950), first Earl Wavell, was educated at Winchester College and is buried in the college chapel.

HEREFORDSHIRE

BREDWARDINE

The diarist **(Robert) Francis Kilvert** (1840-79) was rector at the church of St Andrew from 1877 until his death in 1879. His grave in the churchyard is marked by a white marble cross.

HERTFORDSHIRE

ALDBURY

From 1892 until her death the novelist and social worker Mary Augusta Ward (1851-1920), better known as **Mrs Humphry Ward**, lived at Stocks House, less than a mile (about a kilometre) north of Aldbury. She is buried in the churchyard of St John the Baptist, near the north-west corner of the church.

AYOT ST LAWRENCE

The playwright **George Bernard Shaw** (1856-1950) lived at Shaw's Corner in Ayot St Lawrence from 1906 until his death and wrote in the summerhouse at the

The grave of Francis Kilvert at St Andrew in Bredwardine; there is also a Kilvert memorial bench near the main gate of the churchyard. Kilvert kept his famous diary from 1870 until his death in 1879. It was never intended for publication, and his wife, whom he had married only five weeks before his death, destroyed much of it. A selection from the diary was finally published in 1938-40; it gives a wonderful picture of life in the Welsh borders.

George Bernard Shaw's house, Shaw's Corner in Ayot St Lawrence. Shaw lived there from 1906 until his death in 1950; his ashes and those of his wife, Charlotte Payne-Townshend, who died in 1943, were scattered in the garden. The early twentieth-century house is now in the care of the National Trust and is open to the public.

bottom of the garden. His ashes were scattered in the garden.

HARPENDEN

The comedian **Eric Morecambe** (1926-84) was born in Morecambe as (John) Eric Bartholomew. He was a director of Luton Town Football Club during 1969-75. His ashes were scattered in the garden of remembrance by the church of St Nicholas.

HATFIELD

The novelist **Lady Caroline Lamb** (1785-1828) and her husband Henry William Lamb (1779-1848), second **Viscount Melbourne**, were buried in a vault in the church of St Etheldreda, near Hatfield House. Viscount Melbourne, a Whig politician, was prime minister in 1834 and 1835-41. He has a memorial in the church, but there is no mention of his wife, from whom he separated in 1825 following her public infatuation with the poet Byron.

PERRY GREEN

The sculptor **Henry Moore** (1898-1986), who lived at Hoglands in Perry Green, is buried in the village churchyard.

RIDGE

The soldier **Harold Rupert Leofric George Alexander** (1891-1969), first Earl Alexander of Tunis, Supreme Allied

The grave of the soldier Earl Alexander of Tunis and his wife Margaret in the churchyard of St Margaret at Ridge, Hertfordshire. This tombstone illustrates the late twentieth-century approach to funerary monuments, less flamboyant and more conservative in comparison with the enjoyable excesses of Victorian and Edwardian cemeteries.

Commander in the Mediterranean in 1945, is buried at St Margaret in Ridge, a few miles south-east of Tyttenhanger, his family home. To the right of the path leading to the church porch is his grave, marked by a large, flat ledger, on which he is referred to as 'Alex', the name by which he was known to his friends and soldiers.

ST ALBANS
The Lord Chancellor **Francis Bacon** (1561-1626), first Baron Verulam and Viscount St Albans, lived in St Albans from 1621 until his death, having inherited Gorhambury, a house 2 miles (3 km) to the west. He is buried in St Michael's church, on the north side of the chancel, where there is a life-size marble monument.

SHENLEYBURY
The architect **Nicholas Hawksmoor** (1661-1736) lived near Shenley at Porters Park. He was buried in a plain tomb in the churchyard of St Botolph, Shenleybury, which stands a mile (1.5 km) north of the village of Shenley. The church of St Botolph is now a private residence, and part of the churchyard is a private garden (no access except by prior permission). Also buried there is the racing driver **(Norman) Graham Hill** (1929-75), who died in a flying accident at Arkley, about 3 miles (5 km) south-east of Shenley. Graham Hill was Formula 1 world champion in 1962 and 1968 and is the only driver ever to achieve the triple crown of Formula 1 world championship, Indianapolis and Le Mans.

ISLE OF WIGHT
Soon after the cremation service, the ashes of the writer **Herbert George Wells** (1866-1946) were scattered from an aircraft flying over the English Channel, just west of the Isle of Wight, by his sons Anthony West and Gip Wells.

BONCHURCH
The poet **Algernon Charles Swinburne** (1837-1909) spent his childhood at Bonchurch. He is buried in the graveyard of the new church of St Boniface.

KENT
BECKENHAM
At Beckenham Cemetery, Elmers End Road, a plan on the notice board pinpoints a number of famous graves, all on the north side of the cemetery. The cricketer **William Gilbert (W. G.) Grace** (1848-1915), who died at Eltham, has a bright white marble cross and pedestal and a plaque on his grave showing bat, ball and stumps. Close by is that of **Frederick York Wolseley** (1837-99) with a modern black marble headstone stating 'Inventor of sheepshearing machinery in Australia and producer of the first motor car in England'. Also here are the coffin tomb of **Thomas Crapper** (1837-1900), the London plumber who perfected the design of the water closet, and the grave of **William Walker** (1869-1918), the diver whose work on the foundations of Winchester Cathedral earned him a statue there. Also at Beckenham cemetery is **Lieutenant Colonel Frank Edward Bourne OBE, DCM** (1855-1945), believed to be the last survivor of the battle of Rorke's Drift (1879).

BIRCHINGTON
At All Saints' church, next to the south porch, is the grave of the painter and poet **Dante Gabriel Rossetti** (1828-82), who died at Birchington. His tomb was designed by Ford Madox Brown.

CANTERBURY
Two Archbishops of Canterbury, **Lanfranc** (1005?-89) and **St Anselm** (1033-1109), were buried in Canterbury Cathedral – Lanfranc in St Martin's Chapel and St Anselm in St Anselm's Chapel. The shrine of **St Thomas à Becket** (1118?-70), the

A detail from Rossetti's monument, designed by Ford Madox Brown, whose work was much influenced by the Pre-Raphaelite Brotherhood, or PRB, although he was never actually a member. Rossetti took lessons from Brown for a few months in 1848, then set up the PRB, with six other artists, in 1849.

This granite headstone in Canterbury City Cemetery marks the grave of the author Joseph Conrad. In 1894, after twenty years at sea, Conrad settled in England and turned to writing, publishing his first book at the age of thirty-eight. He initially lived in London but then tried Essex, where he found village life unstimulating, and eventually moved to Kent in 1898.

Archbishop of Canterbury who was murdered in the cathedral, was broken up in 1538. However, his head was reputedly preserved near or under the Corona ('Becket's Crown') at the most easterly point of the cathedral. Edward (1330-76), known as the **Black Prince**, is buried in a splendid tomb on the south side of the cathedral's Trinity Chapel; the tombs of **Henry IV** (1367-1413), king of England, and his queen, **Joan of Navarre** (1370?-1437), are also in the Trinity Chapel. The composer **Orlando Gibbons** (1583-1625) was also buried in the cathedral, while the ashes of the author **William Somerset Maugham** (1874-1965), who was educated at King's School in the cathedral precincts, were placed in the wall of the Maugham Library; a small plaque marks the site.

In the city cemetery, Whitstable Road, is the grave of **Joseph Conrad** (1857-1924), originally Theodor Josef Konrad Korzeniowski, master mariner and novelist. Conrad lived at Orlestone, a few miles south of Ashford, during 1910-19, then moved to the rectory at Bishopsbourne, just south of Canterbury, where he lived until his death in 1924. He is buried in the 'N' section of the cemetery: turn right through the gates and follow the path to one o'clock; he has a tall, rough granite headstone.

A plaque in the St Nicholas Chapel of St Dunstan's church supposedly marks the burial spot of the head of **St Thomas More** (1478-1535), Lord Chancellor. After his execution, his body was buried in St Peter ad Vincula, Tower of London, while the head, after exhibition on London Bridge, was interred in the Roper family vault at St Dunstan's by More's daughter, Margaret Roper. The chapel has a memorial and two commemorative windows.

At the church of St Martin are the graves of **Mary Tourtel** (1874-1948), creator of 'Rupert Bear', and her husband **Herbert Bird Tourtel** (1874-1931), deputy editor of the *Daily Express*. They stand on the raised terrace in the far north-east corner of the graveyard. Also at St Martin is the grave of the artist **Thomas Sidney Cooper** (1803-1902). Cooper, who was born in Canterbury, was nicknamed 'Cow' Cooper as his paintings were almost exclusively of cattle and sheep. He died at Vernon Hulme, near Canterbury, and his grave is a chain-surrounded slab at the corner of paths, 35 yards (32 metres) north of the church.

At St Augustine's Abbey, in the ruins of the St John the Baptist Chapel, are the remains of **Eadbald** (d.640) king of Kent, and three other Anglo-Saxon kings.

CROCKHAM HILL

The philanthropist and co-founder of the National Trust **Octavia Hill** (1838-1912) had a home just outside the village of Crockham Hill, on the edge of the North Downs, from 1884. Her cottage, which had a magnificent view over the Kent and Sussex countryside to the south, was called Larksfield. Octavia Hill was buried in the local churchyard at her own request, although a Westminster Abbey funeral had been offered. She lies with her sisters to the right of the path to the south porch. Her recumbent marble effigy was erected by the altar inside the church in 1928.

DARTFORD

Richard Trevithick (1771-1833), 'father of the locomotive engine', was buried in Holy Trinity churchyard. In his later years he lived in poverty and took lodgings in Dartford when employed upon some of his inventions in the workshop of John Hall. He would have been buried at the expense of the parish had not the workers at Hall's factory clubbed together to give the 'great inventor' a decent funeral. The churchyard is now a public garden.

FARNBOROUGH

In the church of St Giles the Abbot is the grave of the Egyptologist and physicist **Thomas Young** (1773-1829), who assisted with the deciphering of the Rosetta Stone. He was the first to describe astigmatism and to explain colour sensation in the eye.

The statue of the native American princess Pocahontas in the churchyard of St George at Gravesend, which may be her burial place; there are also two memorial windows inside the church.

FOLKESTONE

The author **Colin MacInnes** (1914-76), whose best-known novel is *Absolute Beginners* (1957), in which he described London's Bohemian underworld, was buried at sea off Folkestone. He lived at Hythe, just west of Folkestone, in the period immediately before his death.

GILLINGHAM

James Jershom Jezreel (1840-85), originally James White, founded the 'New and Latter House of Israel' in 1876. He moved to Gillingham in the early 1880s and settled at The Woodlands, which became the headquarters of the Jezreelites. He died at The Woodlands and was buried in Gillingham cemetery.

GRAVESEND

In the grounds of St George's church is a statue of **Pocahontas** (1595-1617), the American Indian princess who became a Christian and married John Rolfe; she came to England in 1616 and died at Gravesend. St George's is supposed to be her burial place, but the exact site of her grave is unknown.

LYMPNE

The tall cross at the south-east corner of the churchyard of St Margaret marks the grave of **Margaret Damer Dawson** (1875-1920), Chief Officer and founder of the Women's Police Service.

OLD ROMNEY

The film director **Derek Jarman** (1942-94) moved to Dungeness in 1987 and used his love of flowers and plants to create what became a famous garden in a most unlikely situation. He was buried beneath a yew tree in the churchyard of St Clement.

PEMBURY

The contractor and politician **Sir Samuel Morton Peto** (1809-89), baronet, died at his home, Blackhurst, in Tunbridge Wells and was buried at Pembury Old Church, 2 miles (3 km) to the north-east. He and his wife Sarah share a large, kerbed grave with double headstone to the east of the south porch.

45

A. W. N. Pugin, who designed the interiors of the Houses of Parliament, is buried in the church he built next to his home at Ramsgate.

RAMSGATE

The architect, ecclesiologist and sailor **Augustus Welby Northmore Pugin** (1812-52) built his home, The Grange at Ramsgate, in 1843-4. He also built the Catholic church of St Augustine, which was attached to the house, during 1844-50. He was buried in the Pugin vault beneath the family chantry chapel in the south transept of St Augustine, in a splendid tomb-chest designed by his son Edward Welby Pugin.

ST MARY IN THE MARSH

The author **Edith Nesbit** (1858-1924), or Mrs Hubert Bland, was best known for her children's books, which included *The Railway Children* (1906). E. Nesbit spent many holidays at Jesson St Mary, near Dymchurch, and died there in 1924. She is buried on the south side of the nearby churchyard at St Mary in the Marsh, her grave marked by a wooden graveboard.

SALTWOOD

The art historian **Kenneth Mackenzie Clark** (1903-83), Baron Clark, who made the BBC television series *Civilisation* in 1969, bought the medieval Saltwood Castle in 1953. He was buried in the nearby churchyard of St Peter and St Paul.

TROTTISCLIFFE

The artist **Graham Vivian Sutherland** (1903-80) and his wife, whose home for many years was at Trottiscliffe, are buried in the churchyard of St Peter and St Paul. The grave is north of the chancel, in the shade of an ancient yew tree.

LANCASHIRE

BOLTON

In the churchyard of St Peter's Parish church is the grave of **Samuel Crompton** (1753-1827), the inventor of the spinning-wheel. He lived at Hall i th' Wood at Tonge, where he created his invention. The granite table tomb that now marks his grave was erected in 1861, paid by subscriptions from textile workers.

LIVERPOOL

The statesman **William Huskisson** (1770-1830), MP for Liverpool 1823-30, was the first person to die in a railway accident. He stepped from a carriage at Newton-le-Willows on the ceremonial opening day of the Liverpool & Manchester Railway and was run down by another train hauled by the *Rocket*. He is buried in the rotunda at St James's cemetery, St James Road.

Robert Noonan (1870?-1911), who wrote as **Robert Tressell**, was an Irish house-painter who produced the manuscript of *The Ragged Trousered Philanthropists* while working in Hastings. He died of tuberculosis in Liverpool in 1911, and his daughter published the book in 1914. Noonan was buried in a paupers' grave with twelve other people in Walton Park cemetery, Hornby Road, Walton; the grave is marked by a marble slab.

MANCHESTER

The chemist and philosopher **John Dalton** (1766-1844) was professor of mathematics and natural philosophy at New College, Manchester, during 1793-9 and president of the Manchester Philosophical Society from 1817 until his death in 1844. He was buried at the old Ardwick cemetery, at the intersection of Hyde Road with Devonshire Street; this has now been redeveloped and the site of the grave is lost.

The artist **Laurence Stephen Lowry** (1887-1976), famous for his northern industrial landscapes, led a secret life as a rent collector in Manchester from 1910 until 1952. He received the freedom of Salford in 1965 and was buried at the Manchester Southern Cemetery, Barlow Moor Road. Here too is the grave of **Sir Matthew 'Matt' Busby** (1909-94), manager of Manchester United Football Club 1945-69, general manager 1969-71, and president 1980-94. He is buried in the Busby family plot.

ROCHDALE

John Bright (1811-89), cotton manufacturer and Liberal MP, was the son of a Rochdale miller. He worked in his father's mill before pursuing his political career. He was buried at the Friends' meeting house in George Street.

SALFORD

Sir Charles Hallé (1819-95), pianist and conductor, settled in Manchester and founded the Hallé Orchestra in 1857. He was buried at the Catholic cathedral in Chapel Street.

LEICESTERSHIRE

LEICESTER

The statesman **Cardinal Thomas Wolsey** (1475?-1530) died in Leicester while on his way to London and was interred in the Lady Chapel of Leicester Abbey. The abbey eventually became ruinous, and, although a memorial slab may be found in the Abbey Park today, the exact site of the grave is unknown.

Richard III (1452-85), king of England, was also buried at Leicester, possibly at the abbey but more probably in the church of the Grey Friars. His remains were later said to have been disinterred and thrown into the river Soar.

The travel agent **Thomas Cook** (1808-92), who organised the first publicly advertised railway excursion in England, was buried at Welford Road cemetery. Cook moved to Leicester in 1841, working as a printer while expanding his travel business, which was booming by the mid 1850s. He died at his home, Thorncroft, 244 London Road, Leicester. His grave, surrounded by a low balustrade, was renovated in 1975 by Thomas Cook & Company.

LUTTERWORTH

The body of the religious reformer **John Wycliffe** (d.1384) was buried in St Mary's churchyard, then disinterred in 1428, burnt, and the ashes thrown in the river Swift as a calculated act of religious desecration. Wycliffe had come to Lutterworth as rector in 1382 after being banned from preaching at Oxford because of his controversial doctrinal views.

LINCOLNSHIRE

STAMFORD

The conductor and composer **Sir (Henry) Malcolm (Watts) Sargent** (1895-1967), who was born in Stamford and educated at Stamford School, was buried at Stamford cemetery, Casterton Road. His marble cross is inscribed with the 'Promenader's Prayer'. To find it, take the drive from the entrance, follow the left-hand bend and, at a footpath crossing, the grave is on the left.

The popular conductor Sir Malcolm Sargent lies in Stamford Cemetery. The inscription on the kerbing says that he was a freeman of Huddersfield, a town with a great choral tradition.

Daniel Lambert (1770-1809), keeper of Leicester gaol and England's fattest man, was staying at the Waggon and Horses Inn in Stamford when he died; his visit was part of a money-making tour. On his death he weighed 739 pounds or nearly 53 stone (335 kg). He was buried in the churchyard of St Martin's, Stamford Baron. Walk through the graveyard behind St Martin's, turn right and cross the road to the graveyard extension. Lambert's grave is marked by slate head and foot stones on the right of the main path.

LONDON

(includes all places with a London Postal District number, listed alphabetically by conventional locality.)

BARNES

The poet and critic **Francis Turner Palgrave** (1824-97), who was brought up in London and published his anthology *The Golden Treasury* in 1861, was buried at Barnes Common cemetery, off Rocks Lane, Barnes, SW13 (take the by-road signed to the Tennis Centre). The cemetery is neglected, vandalised and overgrown. Palgrave's grave is obscured.

BATTERSEA

Henry Saint-John (1678-1751), first Viscount Bolingbroke, statesman, is buried in the family vault at St Mary, Battersea Church Road; the vault is no longer marked, but there is a bust on the north side of the gallery.

BLOOMSBURY

The skeleton of **Jeremy Bentham** (1748-1832), political theorist, is kept at University College, Gower Street, which was founded under the influence of Bentham's educational philosophy.

BRONDESBURY

Arthur Orton (1834-98), the Tichborne claimant, died in poverty in Marylebone and was buried in an unmarked grave in Paddington Cemetery, Willesden Lane, Brondesbury, NW2.

The massive tomb of John Bunyan (1628-88), starkly white after a recent restoration, dominates the former dissenters' burial ground at Bunhill Fields, City Road, London. After publishing 'Pilgrim's Progress' in 1678 he preached in many places, but especially in London.

BUNHILL FIELDS

The grave of **John Bunyan** (1628-88), preacher and writer, may be found at the former Dissenters' burial ground at Bunhill Fields, City Road. His white chest tomb, showing bas-reliefs from *Pilgrim's Progress*, is south-east of the attendant's office and was restored in 1862, when the recumbent effigy was added. The obelisk (north of the attendant's office) commemorating the journalist and novelist **Daniel Defoe** (1661?-1731) was erected in 1870; it was paid for by children's subscriptions, obtained through an appeal in *Christian World*. **William Blake** (1757-1827), writer, artist and visionary, was also buried at Bunhill Fields, but his monument (just north-east of Defoe's obelisk) does not mark the grave, the location of which is unknown. **Mrs Eleanor Coade** (1733-1821), inventor and manufacturer of Coade stone, was also buried at Bunhill Fields along with other members of her family.

CHELSEA

In the church of St Mary, Cadogan Street, is the grave of **Madame Marie Tussaud**, née Gresholtz (1760-1850), founder of the waxwork exhibition, who came to England in 1800 and eventually settled in Baker Street, London. Memorials to her and other members of the Tussaud family are in the south chapel.

CHINGFORD

The East End gangster **Ronnie Kray** (1933-95), one of the notorious and feared Kray twins (the other is Reg Kray), whose heyday was the 1960s, died in Broadmoor hospital. After a service at St Matthew's church, Bethnal Green, Kray's coffin was taken to Chingford on a hearse drawn by six black-plumed horses and followed by twenty-five limousines; crowds lined the streets of the East End to watch the cortège pass by. Ronnie Kray was buried at Chingford Mount Cemetery, Old Church Road, beneath a black polished granite headstone in a plot next to those of his parents, Violet and Charles.

The body of the sculptor **John Bacon** (1740-99) also lies at Chingford Mount Cemetery. He was originally buried in a nonconformist plot, the Whitefield Tabernacle burial ground on Tottenham Court Road, W1, from which many coffins were removed to Chingford in 1898 as the graveyard was in disarray.

CHISWICK

The ashes of **Michael Henry Flanders** (1922-75), actor and lyricist, were scattered in the grounds of Chiswick House, Burlington Lane, Chiswick, where he had enjoyed sitting on summer days.

Although there is no monument to her presence, **Barbara Villiers** (1641-1709), Countess of Castlemaine and Duchess of Cleveland, mistress of Charles II, was buried in St Nicholas, Church Street, Chiswick. **William Hogarth** (1697-1764), the painter and engraver, was buried in the churchyard of St Nicholas (the Hogarth family vault was built later, above his coffin); his monument is an urn on a tall pedestal, with an epitaph by Garrick. Also in the churchyard is the grave of the architect **William Kent** (1684-1748), the protégé of the third Earl of Burlington, who was the designer of Chiswick House. Kent was brought back from Rome to England by Burlington, with whom he lived for the rest of his life.

The tomb of the painter **James Abbott McNeill Whistler** (1834-1903) lies in Chiswick Old Cemetery, Corney Road, W4, which is an extension of the graveyard of St Nicholas. Whistler's Renaissance-style bronze sarcophagus stands against the north wall of the cemetery but now lacks its original four corner statuettes.

The table tomb of the artist James Abbott McNeill Whistler and his wife Beatrix (d.1896), which stands against the north wall of Chiswick Old Cemetery, near St Nicholas's church. The bronze sarcophagus has a dark green granite base; its four corner statuettes have been stolen.

Horatio Nelson's tomb in the crypt of St Paul's Cathedral. The immense black marble sarcophagus was originally intended for the tomb of Cardinal Thomas Wolsey at Windsor; it was made in 1524-9 by Benedetto da Rovezzano. However, when Wolsey died in 1530, he had fallen from royal favour and was buried in Leicester. The unused sarcophagus, having lain for some time in the grave of Jane Seymour beneath St George's Chapel in Windsor, was eventually adapted for Nelson's remains.

CITY OF LONDON

St Paul's Cathedral

Amongst those buried in the original St Paul's Cathedral, which was burnt down in the Great Fire of London in 1666, were **Ethelred II** (968-1016), called the Unready, king of England; **John of Gaunt** (1340-99), Duke of Lancaster, whose tomb was destroyed during the Commonwealth; the painter **Sir Anthony Van Dyck** (1599-1641), who died at Blackfriars; **John Donne** (*c*.1572-1631), poet and divine, whose monument survived and stands in the south aisle of the choir; and **Sir Philip Sidney** (1554-86), soldier, statesman and poet.

In the far south-east corner of the crypt of the new cathedral lies the body of its architect, **Sir Christopher Wren** (1632-1723), under a raised dark slab. His grave is just to the rear of Artists' Corner; a plate on the floor marks the grave of **Sir John Everett Millais** (1829-96), while just to the right is that of the portrait painter **Sir Joshua Reynolds** (1723-92). Nearby is a granite memorial commemorating the Pre-Raphaelite painter **William Holman Hunt** (1827-1910), and also here are the painter and critic **Henry (Johann Heinrich) Fuseli** (1741-1825), the animal painter **Sir Edwin Henry Landseer** (1802-73) and the landscape painter **Joseph Mallord William Turner** (1775-1851).

The Duke of Wellington's huge sarcophagus in the crypt of St Paul's Cathedral was carved from ruddy brown Cornish porphyry by F. C. Penrose. Wellington's magnificent canopied monument was designed by the sculptor Alfred Stevens in 1858-75.

Towards the east end of the crypt are **Sir Henry Maximilian 'Max' Beerbohm** (1872-1956), author and cartoonist, and the artist **Frederic Leighton** (1830-96), Baron Leighton of Stretton, who has an elaborate monument. The ashes of **Walter John De La Mare** (1873-1956), poet and novelist, and **Sir Edwin Landseer Lutyens** (1869-1944), architect, were placed nearby. In the north-east corner of the crypt is a bronze plaque for the composer **Sir Arthur Seymour Sullivan** (1842-1900), who wrote a series of comic operas in collaboration with the librettist W. S. Gilbert; to the left of Sullivan is a white marble tablet marking the grave of **Sir Alexander Fleming** (1881-1955), the bacteriologist who discovered penicillin.

In the centre of the crypt is the splendid tomb of **Horatio Nelson** (1758-1805), Viscount Nelson, vice-admiral, comprising a huge casket raised on a plinth. **John Rushworth Jellicoe** (1859-1935), first Earl Jellicoe, admiral of the fleet, lies alongside Nelson, while nearby is the tomb of **David Beatty** (1871-1936), first Earl Beatty, admiral of the fleet. Just in the nave is the imposing sarcophagus of Arthur Wellesley (1769-1852), first **Duke of Wellington**, field marshal.

Sir Arthur Sullivan

This photograph of Lord Leighton was taken on his appointment as president of the Royal Academy in 1892.

Also buried in the crypt were the orientalist **Edward Henry Palmer** (1840-82), who was murdered by Arab robbers while interpreter-in-chief to the English forces in Egypt; the composer **Sir Charles Hubert Hastings Parry** (1848-1918), baronet; the civil engineer **John Rennie** (1761-1821) and **Sir George Williams** (1821-1905), the founder of the Young Men's Christian Association. The ashes of the painter **Sir Alfred James Munnings** (1878-1959) also lie in the crypt.

City churches

The merchant and philanthropist **Thomas Coram** (1668?-1751) is buried in the small chapel at the west end of St Andrew Holborn, Shoe Lane, Holborn Circus, while the site of the grave of the poet **Thomas Chatterton** (1752-70) is behind the church, under what is now Farringdon Street. This was originally the Shoe Lane Workhouse burial ground. Chatterton came to London in 1770, lodging in Shoreditch and Holborn, and poisoned himself in desperation at his poverty.

Inside St Andrew Undershaft, Leadenhall Street, is the grave of the antiquary **John Stow** (1525?-1605); his monument is a marble and alabaster bust, erected by his wife, which shows him writing in a book with a quill pen. At an annual ceremony, Stow is given a new quill.

The architect **Inigo Jones** (1573-1652) was buried with his parents at St Benet, Paul's Wharf; the colourful **Mrs Mary De La Riviere Manley** (1663-1724), author of *The New Atalantis* (1709), was also buried here.

Richard Lovelace (1618-58), the poet who wrote the song 'Stone walls do not a prison make' in 1642 while imprisoned, died in Shoe Lane and was buried in St Bride, Bride Lane, off Fleet Street. The pickpocket and fortune-teller Mary Frith (1584?-1659), known as **Moll Cutpurse**, was the daughter of a Barbican shoe-maker; she was the heroine of Middleton and Dekker's 1611 comedy *The Roaring Girl*. She died at her home in Fleet Street and was also buried at St Bride, as was the composer **Thomas Weelkes** (*c*.1575-1623). The church was burnt during the Great Fire in 1666, and no trace of these graves remains. **Samuel Richardson** (1689-1761), the novelist, who published *Pamela* in 1740 and lived at nearby Salisbury Court, was buried at St Bride after its reconstruction.

The church of St Giles Cripplegate, Fore Street, was gutted during the Second World War but was reconstructed and now stands within the Barbican complex. The

A bust of the antiquary John Stow in St Andrew Undershaft; the effigy was placed at the grave by Stow's widow. At first Stow was a tailor by trade, but he began to collect and transcribe manuscripts from about 1564. His 'Survey of London' was published in 1598 and 1603.

exact site of the grave of the poet **John Milton** (1608-74), who died nearby and was buried beside his father, has therefore been lost. (There is a statue of Milton in the church.) **Sir Martin Frobisher** (1535?-94), the navigator, was also buried at St Giles, as was the cartographer **John Speed** (1552?-1629), who settled nearby in Moorfields. Speed's bust was damaged during the war but restored in 1970.

 Sir Thomas Gresham (1519?-79), the founder of the Royal Exchange, was buried at St Helen, Bishopsgate; so too was **Robert Hooke** (1635-1703), the inventor and architect.

 Miles Coverdale (1488-1568), translator of the Bible, was rector of St Magnus the Martyr, Lower Thames Street, during 1563-6; he is buried in the church, where there is a memorial.

 Somewhere in the foundations of St Mary Aldermanbury may possibly be the remains of **George Jeffreys** (1644-89), first Baron Jeffreys of Wem, the notoriously brutal judge. He is said to have been buried beneath the altar of the church, which was damaged by bombing during the war and taken down in the 1960s.

 Richard 'Dick' Whittington (d.1423), Mayor of London, was buried at St Michael Paternoster Royal, College Street, EC4; he was a generous benefactor and left a legacy to the church of St Michael.

 At St Olave, Hart Street, Seething Lane, is the tomb of the diarist **Samuel Pepys** (1633-1703), who was Secretary of the Admiralty until 1689, after which he lived in retirement, mainly at Clapham; his memorial overlooks the communion table. For many years Pepys lived just north of the church in Seething Lane, near the Navy Office, and attended St Olave with his wife, with whom he shares his grave in the crypt.

 Roger Ascham (1515-68), tutor to Queen Elizabeth I, is buried at St Sepulchre, Holborn Viaduct, while in the Musicians' Chapel are the ashes of **Sir Henry Joseph Wood** (1869-1944), conductor and founder of the annual Promenade Concerts, who played the organ at the church. Here too, in the south aisle, is the grave of the soldier **Captain John Smith** (1580-1631), rescued from imprisonment in Virginia by the Indian princess Pocahontas, whose grave is said to be at Gravesend, Kent.

 The dramatist and architect **Sir John Vanbrugh** (1664-1726) was buried in the north aisle of St Stephen Walbrook.

 In the small raised court on the north side of the Temple church is the tomb of the author **Oliver Goldsmith** (1730?-74); its approximate site is marked by a clearly

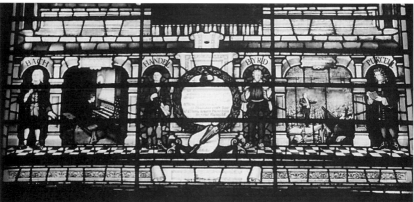

The Musicians' Window in the centre of the Musicians' Chapel at the church of St Sepulchre. This post-Second World War window, dedicated to St Cecilia and designed by Gerald Smith, includes images of Bach, Handel, Byrd, Purcell and two vignettes of Sir Henry Wood playing the organ and conducting. Wood's ashes lie just below the window.

inscribed coffin stone. From 1764 Goldsmith's home was the Temple, although he spent several periods in the country.

COVENT GARDEN
   Harold I (d.1040), king of the English, was originally buried on the site of Westminster Abbey. His body was then disinterred, be-headed and thrown in a fen before reburial in St Clement Danes, Strand; the exact location of the grave is unknown, as the church was rebuilt after bombing during the Second World War. **Thomas Otway** (1652-85), the dramatist, was also buried here.

Robert Boyle

   Because of a rebuilding of St Martin-in-the-Fields, St Martin's Place, during the 1720s, the exact locations of the graves of the first English miniature painter **Nicholas Hilliard** (1537-1619), who died in the parish, the dramatist **George Farquhar** (1678-1707), the natural philosopher **Robert Boyle** (1627-91), who proved experimentally the relationship between elasticity and pressure known as Boyle's Law, and **Eleanor ('Nell') Gwyn** (1650-87), the actress and mistress of Charles II, have been lost. **Thomas Chippendale** (1718-79), the furniture maker who worked in St Martin's Lane, was also buried at St Martin-in-the-Fields.

   Those buried in St Paul's church, Covent Garden (rebuilt following a fire in 1795), include the wood-carver **Grinling Gibbons** (1648-1720), the dramatist **William Wycherley** (1640?-1716), the satirist **Samuel Butler** (1612-80), the portrait painter **Sir Peter Lely** (1618-80), the caricaturist **Thomas Rowlandson** (1757-1827), and **Thomas Augustine Arne** (1710-78), the composer whose works include the music for 'Rule Britannia' (1740). Only Arne has a memorial, on the north wall. Also here, in the 'theatre church', are the actresses **Dame Edith Mary Evans** (1888-1976), whose ashes were buried to the right of the altar, and **Dame (Alice) Ellen Terry** (1847-1928), whose ashes are in a casket on the south wall. Many famous theatre people have commemorative plaques here.

DEPTFORD
   Christopher Marlowe (1564-93), the dramatist, who died during a fight in a nearby inn, was buried in an unmarked grave in the north-east corner of the churchyard of St Nicholas, Deptford Green. A plaque on the churchyard wall marks the approximate spot, although the exact site is unknown.

DULWICH
   Edward Alleyn (1566-1626), actor and founder of Dulwich College (then known as the College of God's Gift), is buried in the college chapel, College Road.

EAST HAM
   The world champion welterweight boxer **Ted 'Kid' Lewis** (1896-1970), whose real name was Gershon Mendaloff, is buried at the Jewish Cemetery, Sandford Road, East Ham, E6. 'Kid' Lewis was born in Aldgate and educated locally; he began boxing professionally at the Judean Club in Whitechapel.

EDMONTON
   Charles Lamb (1775-1834), essayist and humorist, was buried in the churchyard

of All Saints, beside his sister; his tombstone is in a paved enclosure south-west of the church.

Amongst the tall headstones of the Jewish cemetery, Montagu Road, Edmonton, N18, is the grave of **Samuel Montagu** (1832-1911), first Baron Swaythling, banker and philanthropist, co-founder in 1853 of the firm of Samuel Montagu & Company.

ELTHAM

The author **Richmal Crompton Lamburn** (1890-1969), known as Richmal Crompton, was cremated at Eltham Cemetery, Rochester Way, Eltham, SE9. She taught at Bromley High School for Girls during 1917-24, then concentrated on writing; the 'William' series of thirty-eight stories was published between 1922 and her death in 1969.

FINCHLEY

St Marylebone Cemetery, East End Road, Finchley, N3, was founded in 1854 and much used by the wealthy populace of Marylebone, Hampstead and Highgate. Amongst the graves are those of **Sir (Joseph) Austen Chamberlain** (1863-1937), statesman; **Sir Edmund William Gosse** (1849-1928), author of *Father and Son* (1907), who lived near Regent's Park from 1901 until his death; the scientist **Thomas Henry Huxley** (1825-95); **Dame Fanny Lucy Houston** (1857-1936), philanthropist and eccentric; the conductor **Leopold Anthony Stokowski** (1882-

Below left: *The grey and white mottled granite headstone of the conductor Leopold Stokowski in St Marylebone Cemetery at Finchley; it stands just off East Avenue. The cemetery, founded in 1854 and patronised by the affluent of Marylebone and Hampstead, has some splendid early twentieth-century monuments.*

Below right: *The grave of Little Tich, the comedian who stood only 4 feet (1.2 metres) high, is marked by this white marble memorial on the Central Avenue of St Marylebone Cemetery.*

The Golders Green Crematorium was opened in 1902 by Sir Henry Thompson, Queen Victoria's surgeon and first president of the Cremation Society. The buildings, including four furnaces, a columbarium and chapel, were completed well after the official opening and were designed by the country-house architect Sir Ernest George and his partner Alfred Yeates in Italianate style. By the 1930s Golders Green was responsible for over a quarter of all British cremations.

1977); the entertainer Harry Relph (1867-1928), known as **'Little Tich';** and **Alfred Charles William Harmsworth** (1865-1922), Viscount Northcliffe, journalist and newspaper proprietor.

GOLDERS GREEN

Golders Green Crematorium, Hoop Lane, NW11, was opened in 1902 by the London Cremation Company. Prior to that date, cremations of Londoners had taken place at Brookwood near Woking, Surrey, where Britain's first crematorium had been built. Public prejudice against cremation had gradually been overcome, partly through the advocacy of **William Robinson** (1838-1935), the Irish gardener and writer, who was a director of the London Cremation Company and laid out the grounds at Golders Green. His book *The Wild Garden* (1870) contributed to a revolution in garden design. He was cremated at Golders Green, as were a multitude of the famous, particularly from the arts world. There are commemorative plaques, tablets or caskets for many of them, including William Robinson. Golders Green had also been a cemetery since the late nineteenth century, and **Ivor Novello** (1893-

The memorial stones of comedians Bud Flanagan and Bernie Winters (who used to impersonate Flanagan), who were both cremated at Golders Green. Early commemorative slabs, with varying designs, are set in the cloister walls, while later examples – often simple rectangles of stone or slate, like those shown here – appear on many other walls.

1951), the actor-manager and composer who was born David Ivor Davies, was one of those buried here. His bust overlooks one of the arches within the cloisters.

The actresses **Dame Peggy Ashcroft** (1907-91), **Dame (Esmeralda) Cicely Courtneidge** (1893-1980), **Joyce Irene Grenfell** (1910-79) and **Dame (Agnes) Sybil Thorndike** (1882-1976) were cremated here, as were the bandleaders **Billy Cotton** (1899-1969) and **Victor Marlborough Silvester** (1900-78), and the composers **Eric Coates** (1886-1957) and **Sir Arthur Edward Drummond Bliss** (1891-1975), the singers **Kathleen Mary Ferrier** (1912-53) and **Matt Monro** (1930-85), born Terence Parsons, and pianist **Dame (Julia) Myra Hess** (1890-1965).

The jazz saxophonist, bandleader and club owner **Ronnie Scott** (1927-96), born Ronald Schatt, was also cremated at Golders Green; he grew up in Whitechapel and opened the first Ronnie Scott Club in 1959, moving in 1965 to Frith Street. He ran the club until his sudden death.

Comedians cremated here include the radio star **Thomas Reginald ('Tommy') Handley** (1892-1949), **(Charles) Kenneth Horne** (1907-69), leading light of the BBC radio programme *Round the Horne*, **Richard Henry ('Peter') Sellers** (1925-80), **Bernie Winters** (1932-91), and **Bud Flanagan** (1896-1968), whose real name was Chaim Reeven Weintrop. Writers are represented by the children's author **Enid Mary Blyton** (1897-1968); **Percy Wyndham Lewis** (1882-1957), writer and artist; **Sean O'Casey** (1880-1964), Irish dramatist and author; the critic and biographer **(Giles) Lytton Strachey** (1880-1932); and **Abraham ('Bram') Stoker** (1847-1912), the Irish writer who published *Dracula* in 1897. Stoker's ashes are kept in an urn in the Eastern Columbarium.

Others from the arts world cremated here include **Sir George James Frampton** (1860-1928), sculptor; **Sir Alexander Korda** (1893-1956), film producer; **Anna Pavlova** (1885-1931), ballerina; **Dame Marie Rambert** (1888-1982), ballet direc-

tor; the male impersonator **Vesta Tilley** (1864-1952), born Matilda Alice Powles; **Sir John Tenniel** (1820-1914), the artist who illustrated Lewis Carroll's *Alice* books; the architects **Sir (Edward) Guy Dawber** (1861-1938), **Charles Rennie Mackintosh** (1868-1928), and **Charles Francis Annesley Voysey** (1857-1941); and the playwright **Joe Orton** (1933-67) and his lover and killer **Kenneth Halliwell.**

From business and politics came **Ernest Bevin** (1881-1951), trade union leader and statesman; **Emmanuel, Baron Shinwell** (1884-1986), the long-lived Labour politician; **Arthur Henderson** (1863-

The stark, dark grey marble tombstone of the cellist Jacqueline du Pré in the Jewish cemetery at Golders Green bears her name in gold script; it stands near the path leading left from the Hoop Lane entrance. Although this stone is very simple, there are some huge monuments in the western section of the cemetery.

1935), the Labour leader who was awarded the Nobel Peace Prize in 1934; **Simon Marks** (1888-1964), first Baron Marks of Broughton, retailer and son of the founder of Marks & Spencer Ltd, who registered the 'St Michael' brand name in 1928; and **Israel Moses Sieff** (1889-1972), Baron Sieff, the industrialist who joined the board of Marks & Spencer in 1915.

Also cremated here were **Sir Bernard Henry Spilsbury** (1877-1947), the pathologist who gave evidence at many murder trials; and **Alan John Percivale (A. J. P.) Taylor** (1906-90), the historian and broadcaster.

The ashes of **Sigmund Freud** (1856-1939), the founder of psychoanalysis, may be found in a Greek vase in the Ernest George Mausoleum. This was designed by the architects Sir Ernest George and his partner Alfred Yeates, who were responsible for all the early buildings at Golders Green. The mausoleum has space for 1700 cinerary urns and caskets. Freud's daughter, the psychoanalyst **Anna Freud** (1895-1982), was also cremated at Golders Green. The ashes of **Sir Isaac Pitman** (1813-97), the inventor of phonography (a type of shorthand system), are here too, although he was cremated at St John's, Woking, Surrey.

Opposite Golders Green Crematorium is the Jewish cemetery, Hoop Lane, NW11. It is divided into two, the east side being reserved for Sephardic Jews, commemorated by flat stone slabs, while the west is filled with the monuments of the West London Synagogue. In the western side may be found the graves of the cellist **Jacqueline du Pré** (1945-87) and **(Isaac) Leslie Hore-Belisha** (1893-1957), Baron Hore-Belisha, the politician who introduced 'Belisha beacons' as a road safety measure during his time as Minister of Transport in 1934-7.

GREENWICH
In a mausoleum at the Royal Naval Hospital burial ground, to the south-west of the hospital, lies **Sir Thomas Masterman Hardy** (1769-1839), first baronet, vice-admiral and Nelson's flag-captain.

The medieval church of St Alfege (Greenwich parish church), Greenwich High Road, was rebuilt in the early eighteenth century, but the tomb of **Thomas Tallis** (1510?-85), the musician and composer, is in the vault beneath the new chancel. The tomb of **James Wolfe** (1727-59), the major-general who was shot in battle on the Plains of Abraham above Quebec and died after hearing that his attack had been successful, is also in the crypt, in a family vault beneath 'Canadian Corner'.

An engraving of the painting by Benjamin West depicting the death of General Wolfe at Quebec.

GUNNERSBURY

The film director **Sir Carol Reed** (1906-76), who made *The Third Man* in 1949, is buried at Gunnersbury Cemetery, Gunnersbury Avenue, W4, beside his second wife, the actress **Penelope Ward**. Their graves, well hidden by shrubbery on the corner of D plot by the chapel, are marked by two stones carved with daisies, a reference to the home of Reed's mother, May Pinney, which was known as Daisyfield. Gunnersbury Cemetery has always been a focus for the local Polish community, and this was emphasised in 1976 when the Katyn Memorial was erected to commemorate the 14,500 Polish prisoners of war who disappeared in 1940. The memorial, a black obelisk, is now surrounded by Polish graves, including that of the President of the Republic of Poland in exile during 1986-9, **Kazimierz Sabbat** (1913-89).

HAMPSTEAD

In Hampstead Cemetery in Fortune Green Road, off the Finchley Road, are the graves of the jockey **Frederick Archer** (1857-86), **Dame Gladys Constance Cooper** (1888-1971), actress and theatre manager (in the north section by the public footpath), and **Sir William Randal Cremer** (1838-1908), the peace advocate who was awarded the Nobel Peace Prize in 1903. Also here are **Sebastian Ziani De Ferranti** (1864-1930), the electrical engineer and inventor who established Ferranti Ltd in 1896 (west of the chapel), and **Sir Banister Flight Fletcher** (1866-1953), the architectural historian who published, with his father, *A History of Architecture on the Comparative Method* (1896), which is now in its twentieth edition; his four-columned monument was designed by his son. The horn player **Dennis Brain** (1921-57) is by the northernmost path. Closer to the entrance, at a convergence of paths, is the novelist **Pamela Frankau** (1908-67). West of her is **Marie Lloyd** (1870-1922), the musical artiste. The artist **Catherine ('Kate') Greenaway** (1846-1901) is in the undergrowth, south-west of the chapel, near **Joseph Lister** (1827-1912), first Baron Lister, pioneer of antiseptic surgery.

The old churchyard of St John-at-Hampstead, Church Row, was officially closed in 1878, while a new burial ground was opened on the north side of the church in 1812. In the old churchyard are the graves of the ironmaster **Henry Cort** (1740-800), the Scottish dramatist **Joanna Baillie** (1762-1851), both found by turning right immediately through the gateway (Baillie in a railed tomb), and the landscape painter **John Constable** (1776-1837), who was brought up in Essex but lived in London from 1799 onwards. Take the metalled path left from the tower and follow it to a T junction. Constable's railed chest tomb faces you. Also in the old churchyard

Dennis Brain, the French-horn player, who was killed in a car accident, was buried at Hampstead Cemetery. The cemetery, which was founded in 1876, contains many impressive Victorian monuments and even a few extravagant examples from the inter-war years. However, a cemetery regulation of 1934 specified the height of headstones, leading to stones like Brain's becoming the norm.

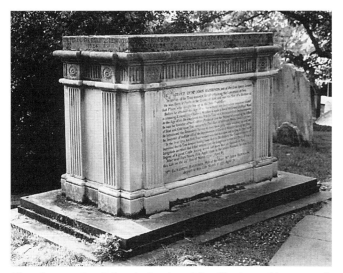

The chest tomb of the clockmaker John Harrison, 'the man who discovered longitude', in the old churchyard of St John, Hampstead. Its inscription, restored by the Worshipful Company of Clockmakers, describes the invention of his chronometers. The railings around the tomb were removed in 1934.

lie the architect **Richard Norman Shaw** (1831-1912) – in a tomb-chest by a yew tree – and the horologist **John Harrison** (1693-1776), whose tomb was reconstructed by the Clockmakers' Company in 1879. It is next to the wall of the church.

In the churchyard extension are the graves of the poet and suffragette **Eva Gore-Booth** (1870-1926), the novelist and social reformer **Sir Walter Besant** (1836-1901), the architect **George Gilbert Scott** (1839-97), the author **Eleanor Farjeon** (1881-1965) – close to the north wall, the writer and philosopher **Cyril Edwin Mitchinson Joad** (1891-1953), on the right of the path leading north from the water tank, and, near the cloisters, the editor of *Punch* **Edmund George Valpy Knox** (1881-1971). Also buried next to the cloisters was the Labour politician **Frank Soskice** (1902-79), Baron Stow Hill. The tomb of the **Llewelyn Davies family** is in the south-east corner; the author James Barrie based his children's play *Peter Pan* on stories he made up for the five sons of Arthur and Sylvia Llewelyn Davies, to whom he later gave a home after their parents' death. Also in the churchyard extension, by the railings facing the church, are the graves of the actor **Anton Walbrook** (1900-67), the actress **Kay Kendall** (1927-

The green slate headstone of the actress Kay Kendall (1927-59), third wife of the actor Rex Harrison, stands in the south-east corner of the extension of St John's churchyard, Hampstead. There are several other theatrical graves in this area, including those of Anton Walbrook and Sir Herbert Beerbohm Tree.

61

59) and the author and cartoonist **George Louis Palmella Busson Du Maurier** (1834-96). The ashes of the Labour Party leader **Hugh Todd Naylor Gaitskell** (1906-63) are in an urn which stands on a podium, while the grave of the actor-manager **Sir Herbert Beerbohm Tree** (1852-1917) is graced by the statue of a maiden. Both are by the railings facing the church.

HANWELL

In the crypt of St Mary, Church Road, Hanwell, lies **Jonas Hanway** (1712-86), traveller and philanthropist, pioneer of the umbrella. The crypt is occasionally open on summer Sundays and Hanwell has a memorial plaque on his vault. (The parish magazine is called *The Umbrella*.)

HENDON

Sir Thomas Stamford Raffles (1781-1826), colonial governor in the service of the East India Company, was buried at St Mary, Hendon; he returned to England in 1824 and lived in retirement near Barnet.

At Hendon Cemetery, Holder's Hill Road, Finchley, NW4, is the grave of **Joseph Havelock Wilson** (1858-1929), the founder of the National Union of Seamen. His massive grave ledger, 6 feet 7 inches by 9 feet 10 inches (2 by 3 metres), is on the right as you walk up the main drive.

HIGHGATE

Highgate Cemetery, Swain's Lane, was opened in 1839 to cater for the prosperous inhabitants of north London. It is divided into the old, Western Cemetery and the new, Eastern Cemetery by Swain's Lane. In the Western Cemetery (which is open only to guided tours) are **(Marguerite) Radclyffe Hall** (1880-1943), the novelist who published *The Well of Loneliness* in 1928, and – in the Rossetti family plot – the poet **Christina Georgina Rossetti** (1830-94), sister of Dante Gabriel Rossetti, and **Elizabeth Eleanor Siddal** (1829-62), his wife. She was buried with a manuscript of some of his poems, which he retrieved from her coffin in 1869. Also here are Ellen Wood (1814-87), known as **Mrs Henry Wood**, the novelist whose best-known work was *East Lynne* (1861); Stella Webb (1902-89), who as **Stella Gibbons** wrote *Cold Comfort Farm;* **Jacob Bronowski** (1908-74), the mathematician who filmed the BBC television series *The Ascent of Man* in 1971-2; **Philip Harben** (1906-70), the television cook; **Frederick William Lilywhite** (1792-1854), the cricketer; **Frederick Warne** (1825-1901), the publisher; **Carl Rosa** (1843-89), founder of the opera company; **Peter Robinson** (1804-74), founder of the department store; **John Maple** (1815-1900), founder of the furniture store; **Patrick Wymark** (1926-70), the television actor; **Charles Cruft** (1852-1938), who founded the eponymous dog show in 1886; **George Dalziel** (1815-1902), founder of Dalzial brothers, the most prominent firm of Victorian engravers; **John Copley, Baron Lyndhurst** (1772-1863) thrice Lord Chancellor who led the prosecution of George IV's Queen Caroline; **Edward Bailey** (1788-1867) sculptor of Nelson on his column; **Henry Y. Darracott Scott** (1822-93), who designed the Albert Hall; **Brodie Wilcox** (1785-1862), founder of the P & O Steamship Co; **Michael Faraday** (1791-1867), the natural philosopher who discovered magneto-electricity in 1831; and **Charles Chubb** (1770-1846), locksmith and founder of Chubb & Company. **Eugenius Birch** (1818-84), engineer and seaside architect, designer of Brighton's West Pier, is buried in grave number 25915. The splendid and much visited tomb of the pugilist **Tom Sayers** (1826-65), unbeaten middleweight boxing champion of England, is guarded by a statue of his faithful dog Lion.

Highgate's Eastern Cemetery is open to individual visitors. To the right of the entrance gate is a group of graves that includes **Leslie Hutchinson, 'Hutch'** (1900-69), the cabaret pianist and broadcaster. Take the main drive ahead past **William Alfred Westropp Foyle** (1885-1963), the bookseller who opened a shop in Charing

Cross Road in 1907, and just before a cross way is, on the right, the simple headstone of **Shura Cherkassy** (1911-95), the concert pianist. Turn right and take the next path on the left. On the left is the square pedestal of the organist **Sir George Thomas Thalben-Ball** (1897-1987), with a central depression forming a bird bath and two stone birds beside it. Return to the cross path, turn left past the cross of **Francis 'Frank' Matcham** (1854-1920), the theatre architect, on the right and continue to the gardeners' store. Turn left along the edge of the cemetery to the tall obelisk surmounted by a cross, the grave of **William Friese-Greene** (1855-1921), the pioneer of motion photography. His inscription, to 'the inventor of kinematography', even includes his patent number!

Return to the main drive, turn right and immediately fork left (past the figure of Caroline Tucker), and turn up the second path on the left to the grey granite obelisk of Mary Ann Evans (1819-80), who wrote as **George Eliot**. Beyond her obelisk is the bust of **George Jacob Holyoake** (1817-1906), the secularist who invented the term 'secularism'. Opposite and twenty paces in is the slate headstone of the Australian artist **Sir Sidney Robert Nolan** (1917-92). Return down to the main drive and turn left to the massive square-cut memorial to **Karl Marx** (1818-83), surmounted by his head. Marx settled in London after the 1848 revolutions in Europe. Among the graves between Marx and the perimeter railings is the simple rounded headstone of **Max Wall** (1908-90), the comedian. Return to the main drive fork and turn left down the drive for 100 yards (90 metres) to the grave of the actor **Sir Ralph David Richardson** (1902-83), a simple white ledger on the left. Further down, on the right, is **Sir Eyre Massey Shaw** (1828-1908), chief of the London Fire Brigade, the 'Captain Shaw' invoked by the Fairy Queen in Gilbert and Sullivan's *Iolanthe.*

Up the hill from the cemetery, in Highgate village the poet **Samuel Taylor Coleridge** (1772-1834) was buried in the vault under the centre aisle of St Michael, the parish church; he lived in Highgate from 1816 until his death in 1834. His tombstone reads 'Beneath this sod, A poet lies, or that which once seemed he...'

ISLINGTON

Behind the John Wesley Chapel on City Road, Finsbury (almost opposite Bunhill Fields), is the grave of the Methodist leader **John Wesley** (1703-91), who founded the chapel.

George Fox (1624-91), founder of the Society of Friends, died in London and was buried in the Quaker burial ground at the Friends' meeting house off Banner Street. The burial ground is now a garden and the exact position of the grave is not known but a commemorative stone records Fox's burial here.

Between Cumming Street and Rodney Street, just off to the north of Pentonville Road, N1, is Joseph Grimaldi Park, once the churchyard of St James, where **Joseph Grimaldi** (1778-1837), actor and clown, was buried. His railed tomb, by the east wall of the former church, is adorned with theatrical masks and has an explanatory plaque.

In St Luke, Old Street, Islington, was buried **William Caslon** (1692-1766), the elder, the typefounder who designed the Caslon typeface. St Luke's is now gutted and the churchyard is a public garden.

At the St Pancras and Islington Cemetery, High Road, East Finchley, N12, are the graves of the painter **Ford Madox Brown** (1821-93) and **Ludwig Mond** (1839-1909), chemical manufacturer and art collector. Mond is interred near the centre of the cemetery in the huge Mond mausoleum, a granite temple designed by the architect Darcy Braddell in 1909. Take the main drive from the entrance gate and fork left at the cross road. The mausoleum is on the right at the next junction. Behind this a path leads to Chapel Hill, where Madox Brown's grave is in the undergrowth on the left.

KENSAL GREEN

London's first cemetery – All Souls Cemetery, Harrow Road, Kensal Green, W10 – was consecrated by the Bishop of London on 24th January 1833 and contains a fine array of monuments and mausolea within its 77 acres (31 hectares).

Passing through the main entrance archway on the Harrow Road, walk straight ahead and follow the path which leads towards the Grand Union Canal. As it curves to the left, two tall obelisks come into view: one commemorates Robert Owen (1771-1858), the social reformer (who is not buried here, but at Newtown, Powys); the other is the Reformers' Memorial. This cenotaph commemorates eighty-five social reformers of the nineteenth and twentieth centuries and was restored in 1997, the re-opening ceremony being presided over by the former Labour leader Michael Foot.

Retrace your steps towards the entrance and take the left-hand road, Centre Avenue, which is the main path that runs through the middle of the cemetery. Take the first-right path leading off Centre Avenue, and the headstone to **Mary Scott Hogarth** (1819-1837) may be found 100 yards (90 metres) along on the right, against the wall backing on to the Harrow Road. Her brother-in-law, Charles Dickens, wrote her epitaph. The grave is maintained by the Dickens Fellowship.

Directly south of Hogarth, between Centre Avenue and the Grand Union Canal, the grave of **Feargus O'Connor** (1794-1855), the Chartist leader, may be located. His hexagonal Gothic spire stands to the south of a small path. Walk down to the canalside path (South Avenue); 50 yards (45 metres) further west along that path is a flat slab with railings. It commemorates the novelist **William Makepeace Thackeray** (1811-63). The next grave but one is that of his greatest friend, **John Leech** (1817-64), who illustrated Dickens's works. Opposite these two, in an unmarked plot, lies **Richard Parkes Bonnington** (1802-28), artist and friend of Delacroix. Just further west and in from the path are a small angled headstone and raised ledger to **Andrew Pears** (d.1845), founder of the soap company that still bears his name. Along the next path on the right is a simple marble block to the civil engineers **Isambard Kingdom Brunel** (1806-59) and his father **Sir Marc Isambard**

This solid marble block marks the graves of the Brunel family at Kensal Green Cemetery. Here lie the engineers Sir Marc Isambard Brunel and his son Isambard Kingdom Brunel (left), their wives and other family members. The monument stands just off Centre Avenue, towards its east end.

The tomb of the artist William Mulready, who died in 1863, is one of the more outstanding of Kensal Green Cemetery's amazing collection of funerary architecture. The canopied early Renaissance effigy, made of artificial stone, was designed by Godfrey Sykes and stands on Centre Avenue.

Brunel (1769-1849). Continue westward on Centre Avenue where it becomes a gravel path; the splendid artificial stone Renaissance-style tomb of the genre painter **William Mulready** (1786-1863) can be found 40 yards (37 metres) along on the right-hand side. His recumbent effigy lies under a canopy upon a base showing depictions of his paintings.

Beside Mulready's tomb is a small path. Walk along this until it bisects another path, and turn right. On the left-hand side is a simple headstone to **Dr 'James' Barry** (1795-1865), the first woman doctor, who concealed her sex whilst serving as an army surgeon. Turn back and walk south down to the Centre Avenue again, and the large classical mausoleum of **George Birkbeck** (1776-1841), philanthropist and founder of Birkbeck College, can be found on the right-hand side of the Avenue. Immediately next to Birkbeck is the former grave of the caricaturist George Cruikshank (1792-1878), a red granite pedestal which was originally topped with a bronze bust. Cruikshank's remains were translated to St Paul's Cathedral in 1878.

Walk a short way back down the Centre Avenue to the crossroads with the Circle Avenue. Turn right, and on the outside of the circle path at its south-east point is a grey granite urn on a Portland stone pedestal to **John Claudius Loudon** (1783-1843), the horticulturalist and landscape gardener. Further along is the pink granite obelisk of the composer **Michael William Balfe** (1808-70), composer of *The Bohemian Girl*. Opposite Balfe on the inner side of the circle is the large red granite pedestal to the poet **Thomas Hood** (1798-1845). Author of *The Song of the Shirt*, he once mortgaged his brain for a cash advance. The bronze bust and portrait medallions which once adorned the monument are now missing. Further on, on the inner side of the circle, is a pink granite and marble monument to **Thomas De La Rue** (1793-1866). A familiar name to philatelists, De La Rue was Britain's official printer of postage stamps, banknotes and cheques.

At the southernmost point of the circle, turn north on to Junction Avenue. Halfway up the Avenue and on the right in the sixth row back is the grave of **Ann Isabella Byron** (1792-1860), wife of the poet Lord Byron. This is a grey granite slab with railings. Walk back to Junction Avenue and continue north until it bisects the Centre Avenue. Turn left, and directly in front and to the right of the Anglican Chapel, under a massive Cornish grey granite slab with bollards, lies **HRH the Duke of Sussex** (1773-1843), sixth son of George III and Queen Charlotte. His interment at Kensal Green Cemetery made it a very fashionable place to be buried and ensured the cemetery's future success. Opposite him, a huge marble plinth topped with an ornate marble sarcophagus marks the burial vault of his sister **HRH the Princess Sophia** (1777-1848).

Walk up to the Anglican Mortuary Chapel, and through the colonnaded area behind. Underneath the entire paved area is the subterranean catacomb, which houses nearly three thousand coffins within a series of underground corridors. (There are two other catacombs in Kensal Green cemetery, but these are now inaccessible.) Deposited in the catacombs are **Lady Jane Franklin** (1792-1875), traveller and wife of the North Pole explorer Sir John Franklin; **Sir William Beatty FRS MD** (1793-1842), the naval surgeon who attended Nelson at Trafalgar; **Augusta Leigh** (d.1851), half-sister to Lord Byron; **William Powell Frith CVO RA** (1819-1909), painter of 'Derby Day'; **William Charles Macready** (1793-1873), actor; and **Thomas Wakley FRCS** (1795-1862), medical reformer and founder of *The Lancet*.

Behind the Anglican Chapel on the West Centre Avenue is a small path on the right. Along this path, on the left, is the grave of the novelist **William Wilkie Collins** (1824-89), with a white marble cross on a stepped plinth. Widely considered to be the father of the English detective novel, Collins is buried with one of his mistresses. Go back to the West Centre Avenue; opposite the path to Collins's grave, and a few yards to the west, is the grave of **Charles Blondin** (1824-97), born Jean François Gravelet, the tightrope walker who traversed the Niagara Falls. The red granite monument, topped by a marble female figure, shows Blondin and his wife in bas-relief portrait medallions.

Turn left on a small path a few yards west of Blondin's grave. Go past three mausolea, and on the right lies a red granite ledger with a cross running its length. This commemorates **Anthony Trollope** (1815-82), the novelist and Post Office

Anthony Trollope's tomb, towards the west end of Kensal Green Cemetery, is a disappointing red granite slab with no decoration other than a large cross. The prolific novelist, whose popularity was at its peak in the 1860s, was born in London and stood unsuccessfully for Parliament in 1868. Trollope felt a seat in Parliament should be 'the highest object of ambition to every educated Englishman'.

official credited with inventing the pillar-box. Continue south, following the path as it curves past three junctions; just to the right, before a T-junction, is the grave of the poet **James Henry Leigh Hunt** (1784-1859), a marble plinth once topped with a bust. Continue south to a dirt road and follow it west towards a rubbish tip. Near this tip, in a common grave (unmarked) lies **Lady Jane Francisca 'Speranza' Wilde** (1821-96), mother of Oscar Wilde, wit and dramatist. On the inner curve of this path as it turns north is a large monument in pink and grey granite, with a marble book on top. This is the grave of **William Henry Smith** (1792-1865), whose mother founded the chain of book and stationery shops which still bear his name. Continuing north, take the next left-hand path, going westwards, and a few yards along on the right is the grave of **George Grossmith** (1847-1912), entertainer, marked by a white marble cross. With his brother Weedon, Grossmith published *Diary of a Nobody* in 1894. Continue west, and in front of a small military cemetery on the left is the grave of **Percy Sholto Douglas, ninth Marquess of Queensbury** (1868-1920), brother of Lord Alfred Douglas, the friend of Oscar Wilde. His monument is a marble cross under a simple Gothic canopy.

Walk north across West Centre Avenue, and continue north along the main path towards the north entrance of the cemetery. Near the entrance, and on the junction of Oxford Avenue, is the Rattigan family grave, marked by a large marble cross with a stone trellis surround. The playwright **Sir Terence Mervyn Rattigan** (1911-77) was cremated in Bermuda and his remains were brought back to the family grave.

Also buried at Kensal Green are **William Whiteley** (1831-1907), the store owner who began his career as a draper's assistant and ended as the 'Universal Provider', who was murdered in his own store; **Charles Babbage** (1791-1871), mathematician and inventor of the difference engine; the architects **William Burn** (1789-1870), **Philip Hardwick** (1792-1870) and **Decimus Burton** (1800-81); **Joseph Locke** (1805-60), civil engineer and railway constructor; **John Murray** (1778-1843), publisher; **Thomas Hancock** (1786-1865), founder of the india-rubber trade in England; **Sir William Siemens** (1823-83), the metallurgist and inventor; the cook **Alexis Benoit Soyer** (1809-58); and the actor **Charles Kemble** (1775-1854).

Guided tours take place every Sunday at 2 p.m. from the Anglican Chapel, and on the first Sunday of the month a visit to the catacomb is included.

At St Mary's Roman Catholic Cemetery, Harrow Road, Kensal Green, NW10, are the graves of **Sir John (Giovanni Battista) Barbirolli** (1899-1970), conductor; the broadcaster and television star **Gilbert Charles Harding** (1907-60); **Cardinal Henry Edward Manning** (1808-92); **Louis Wain** (1860-1939), the artist who specialised in cats; and **Sir Anthony Panizzi** (1797-1879), the principal librarian of the British Museum, who conceived the idea of the great reading room.

KENSINGTON

The novelist, dramatist and actress **Elizabeth Inchbald** (1753-1821) was buried in the church previously on the site of St Mary Abbotts, Kensington Church Street, Kensington.

LAMBETH

Part of the churchyard of St Mary, sited between Lambeth and Lambeth Palace Roads, is now a garden run by the Tradescant Trust. It features plants introduced to England by **John Tradescant the elder** (*c.*1570-1638), who was Charles I's gardener, and his son **John Tradescant the younger** (1608-62), who succeeded his father in the post. The Tradescants were naturalists and travellers who lived in south Lambeth, where John the elder established the first physic garden. The church itself is now the Museum of Garden History, while the Tradescants were buried in a sarcophagus which stands in the churchyard to the east of the church; it was erected by the widow of John the younger in 1662, repaired in 1773 and recarved in 1853. The relief design includes a crocodile and other fauna and flora. Nearby is the well-preserved Coade stone sarcophagus of **William Bligh** (1754-1817), mariner and explorer, captain of HMS *Bounty*; his tomb-chest is topped by a flaming urn. Just south of the church, by the porch, is the tomb of the Sealy family, including **John Sealy** (1749-1813). He was the cousin of Mrs Eleanor Coade, inventor and manufacturer of Coade stone, and also her partner at the Coade factory in Lambeth during 1799-1813. The Sealy tomb (in Coade stone) comprises a pedestal topped by an urn with a serpent twisted around it. Also buried at St Mary is **Elias Ashmole** (1617-92),

The sarcophagus topped by an urn is the tomb of the explorer William Bligh, while on the right is the chest tomb of two gardeners: the John Tradescants, father and son; the graves are in the churchyard of St Mary, Lambeth, now a garden. Bligh's tomb is made of hard-wearing Coade stone, while the Tradescants' sarcophagus, recarved in 1853, shows a splendidly arrogant multi-headed griffin, amongst other fauna.

the antiquary who eventually took over the Tradescants' gardens and collections and founded the Ashmolean Museum at Oxford.

LEWISHAM

Sir George Grove (1820-1900), the writer who edited the *Dictionary of Music and Musicians* (1878-89), is buried at Brockley Cemetery, Brockley Road, Lewisham.

In the churchyard of Old St Margaret, Lee Terrace, Lewisham, SE3, which contains many substantial eighteenth- and nineteenth-century monuments, are the graves of two Astronomers Royal: **Edmund Halley** (1656-1742), who observed the comet that bears his name in 1680, and **John Pond** (1767-1836).

MARYLEBONE

The old graveyard of St Mary-le-bone, the parish church at the north end of Marylebone High Street that was demolished in 1949, has been turned into a garden. Those buried here include **Charles Wesley** (1707-88), the divine and hymn writer; the architect **James Gibbs** (1682-1754); **Edmond Hoyle** (1672-1769), the writer on card games; the sculptor **John Michael Rysbrack** (1693?-1770); **George Stubbs** (1724-1806), the anatomist and horse painter; and **Allan Ramsay** (1713-84), the Scottish portrait painter. The graves are all lost although an obelisk commemorates Wesley.

MAYFAIR

In the Grosvenor Chapel, South Audley Street, were buried the writer **Lady Mary Wortley Montagu** (1689-1762), who lived in St George Street during her last months, and the politician **John Wilkes** (1727-97), who lived in Grosvenor Square at the end of his life. He is buried in the vaults.

MORTLAKE

Sir Richard Francis Burton (1821-90), the explorer, flamboyant character and translator of the *Arabian Nights* (1885-8), spent a short time at school in nearby Richmond. He was buried in the Roman Catholic churchyard behind St Mary Magdalen, North Worple Way, Mortlake, in a mausoleum designed by his wife, Lady Isabel Burton. It is a life-size Bedouin tent in Forest of Dean stone. At the back a ladder leads to a window, through which the tomb and coffins of Burton and his wife are visible.

NORWOOD

The picturesque West Norwood Cemetery, Norwood High Street, SE27, opened in 1837 and covers some 40 acres (16 hectares). It is administered by Lambeth Council, which purchased it in 1966. A trail guide to the most interesting monuments is available from the office at the entrance. Take the main drive from the entrance and shortly on the right is the square-cut grey granite tombstone of **Sir Hiram Stevens Maxim** (1840-1916), engineer and inventor of the Maxim gun. Further on on the left is a pedestal surmounted by an urn and drapery over the grave of **Thomas King** (1835-88), the prizefighter. Fork right and continue to the path on the left signed 'Ships Path'. Take this and shortly on the left is the grave of **Sir Henry Bessemer** (1813-98), the metallurgist. When the path crosses another, take the green path left to see on the right the simple headstone of the author of *Household Management*, **Mrs Isabella Beeton** (1836-65), and her publisher husband. Return to the crossing and turn left to reach a metalled drive. To the right is the column (alas without its urn) commemorating **Dr William Marsden** (1796-1867), founder of the Royal Free Hospital. Continue past this to a T-junction and turn left. Shortly on the left, surrounded by holly bushes, is the massive 10 ton ledger of **Thomas Cubitt** (1788-1855), the builder who erected the east front of Buckingham Palace. Continue to the sign 'Doulton Path' and turn left along it. After 60 yards (50

metres), at the pink Sturdy family monument, turn left into the undergrowth for 20 yards (17 metres) to find the coffin tomb of **William Burges** (1827-81), the architect. Designed for his mother and also containing his father, it is, for Burges, comparatively unembellished, with only a floral cross. Return to Doulton Path and continue to the splendid terracotta mausoleum built for **Sir Henry Doulton** (1820-97), restored 1992-7. Doulton, a potter, began work at his family's pottery in Lam-

At Norwood Cemetery stands the terracotta mausoleum of Sir Henry Doulton, the potter, and his son Henry Lewis Doulton. The design is attributed to R. Stark Wilkinson.

The funeral of C. H. Spurgeon at Norwood Cemetery, with an open Bible lying upon the coffin.

beth in 1835 and greatly expanded the business. The path leads to the cemetery chapel. Continue around the right side of it to another terracotta mausoleum, designed by George & Peto for **Sir Henry Tate** (1819-99). Tate was a public benefactor who made his fortune from Tate's cube sugar. He lived at Park Hill, Streatham, and offered his art collection to the nation on condition that a site was found for a new gallery, which he would build. The collection is now housed in the National Gallery of British Art (the Tate Gallery), which opened in 1897. Continue past the Tate mausoleum to the grave of **Charles Haddon Spurgeon** (1834-92), popular preacher and founder of the Metropolitan Tabernacle. His bust decorates his grey sarcophagus. The drive leads back to the entrance.

Also buried here are **Thomas Letts** (1803-73), the bookbinder and originator of 'Letts' Diaries', the social reformer **Eleanor Florence Rathbone** (1872-1946), **Joseph Whitaker** (1820-95), the publisher who began the annual publication of *Whitaker's Almanac* in 1868, **Paul Julius Reuter** (1816-99), founder of the press agency, and **William Edgar** (1791-1869), of the former Piccadilly store Swan & Edgar.

NUNHEAD

At Nunhead Cemetery, Linden Grove, SE15, is the grave of **Sir Charles Fox** (1810-74), the engineer who specialised in railway construction and also produced the working drawings for the 1851 Great Exhibition building from the design of Joseph Paxton.

Sarah Siddons in her role as Lady Macbeth.

PADDINGTON

The actress **Mrs Sarah Siddons** (1755-1831) is buried in the churchyard of St Mary, Paddington Green, at the far north end of the emparked churchyard extension, within railings and under a canopy, out of sight of her memorial statue on the green.

PRIMROSE HILL

The ashes of the composer **(Agnes) Elizabeth Lutyens** (1906-83) were scattered on Primrose Hill.

PUTNEY

In the popular Putney Vale Cemetery, Kingston Road, SW15, with its many monuments of the late nineteenth and early twentieth century, are buried **Sir Jacob Epstein** (1880-1959), the sculptor who settled in London in 1905 (his rough-hewn stone is by the south perimeter); **Sir Edward Hulton** (1869-1925), the newspaper proprietor; **Sir Frederick Thomas George Hobday** (1869-1939), the veterinary surgeon whose successful operation to relieve 'roaring' in horses led to the term 'hobdayed'; **Howard Carter** (1874-1939), the archaeologist who (with the Earl of Carnarvon) discovered the tomb of Tutankhamun (Carter's grave is on the right of the first right-hand path beyond the circle); and **(Francis) Roy Plomley** (1914-85), deviser and presenter of the radio programme *Desert Island Discs*, which was first broadcast in 1942 (his grave faces the south perimeter).

Also buried here were the painter **Sir William Newenham Montague Orpen** (1878-1931) and the shipowner **Joseph Bruce Ismay** (1862-1937), son of the founder of the White Star Line; his tomb, by the south-eastern circle of the cemetery, is carved with three schooners. Also buried by the south perimeter were **Alexander Feodorovich Kerensky** (1881-1970), leader of the provisional government in Russia during 1917, and the crime writer Reginald Evelyn Peter Southouse-Cheyney (1896-1951), usually known as **Peter Cheyney**. **Patrick Robert Reid** (1910-90), who was a German prisoner of war during 1940-2 and published *The Colditz Story* in 1953, is here. The inscription on his headstone reads 'May this last escape

The grave of Alexander Kerensky at Putney Vale Cemetery. Kerensky, who led Russia's provisional government during 1917, eventually escaped the country, travelling through Finland to France and England. He married an Australian journalist in 1939, and the couple lived briefly in Australia before her death in 1945, after which Kerensky went to America. He died in New York in 1970, leaving a son who lived in England.

71

bring you the greatest freedom'. His grave lies on the right of the main drive from the circle to the crematorium.

The footballer **Bobby Moore** (1941-93), who captained England's World Cup winning side of 1966, was cremated at Putney Vale, although his ashes were returned to the East End. Also cremated here were the novelist **Dame Ivy Compton-Burnett** (1884-1969); the billiards and snooker star **Joseph 'Joe' Davis** (1901-78), the actors **Donald Pleasence** (1919-95), **Sir Stanley Baker** (1928-76), **Margaret Mary Lockwood** (1916-90) and **Kenneth Gilbert More** (1914-82), the television personality **Reginald Bosanquet** and the cricketer **Jim Laker** (1923-86). The art historian and spy **Anthony Frederick Blunt** (1907-83) was cremated at Putney, then his ashes were scattered on the Wiltshire Downs near his former home.

ST JOHN'S WOOD

John Sell Cotman (1782-1842), watercolourist, was a drawing-master in Norwich before coming to London in 1834, where he taught until his death in 1842. He was interred in the burial ground (now a garden) of St John's Wood church, Wellington Road; so too was **Joanna Southcott** (1750-1814), the fanatic. By the central entrance in Wellington Place a board gives directions to the graves, which are on the west of the churchyard, Cotman's marked with a modern sign.

ST PANCRAS

In the old churchyard (now a garden) of St Pancras, Pancras Road, were buried **Johann Christian Bach** (1735-82), 'the English Bach', and the architect **Sir John**

In the rather dispiriting surroundings of St Pancras old churchyard, now a garden, stands the elegant tomb of the architect of the Bank of England, Sir John Soane (1753-1837). The domed canopy, which Soane himself designed, hides the entrance to the Soane family vault.

Soane (1753-1837), who had lived in Lincoln's Inn Fields since 1812. Bach's grave is lost but the Soane family tomb, a handsome canopied vault constructed to Soane's own design, stands on an island site to the north of the church, surrounded by a metal guard fence. One of the angled ledgers still surviving commemorates the sculptor **John Flaxman** (1755-1826), buried here, and the elaborate decorated column within rails and stone beasts lists the local notables buried here before the church-yard became a pleasure ground.

SOHO

The essayist **William Hazlitt** (1778-1830) was buried in St Anne's churchyard, Dean Street, while the ashes of **Dorothy Leigh Sayers** (1893-1957), the crime writer who introduced the character Lord Peter Wimsey in 1923, were placed in the small tower chapel. She had been a churchwarden of St Anne's for some years.

At the church of St Giles-in-the-Fields, St Giles High Street, by Charing Cross Road, are the graves of **Andrew Marvell** (1621-78), poet and satirist, and **Luke Hansard** (1752-1828), the printer who produced the House of Commons' *Journals* from 1774. They are commemorated within: Marvell on the north wall and Hansard on one of the pillars. John Flaxman (1755-1826), the sculptor, is commemorated in the porch but his body is at St Pancras. Also commemorated, by the citizens of Maryland, USA, is the second **Lord Baltimore** (1606-75), the first proprietor of Maryland.

SOUTHWARK

The dramatist **John Fletcher** (1579-1625) was buried in the Cathedral of St Saviour and St Mary Overie, London Bridge, but his grave is no longer marked.

STOKE NEWINGTON

At the popular Abney Park Cemetery, Stoke Newington High Street, N16, which filled up rapidly after its opening in 1840, is the grave of **William Booth** (1829-

The headstone in the shape of a shield marks the grave of William Booth, founder of the Salvation Army, at Abney Park Cemetery in Stoke Newington. He shares the grave with his wife, the preacher Catherine Booth (1829-90), 'Mother of the Salvation Army'. Abney Park was established in 1840 for the use of nonconformists; it has many monuments, but none to compare with the lavish statuary of Kensal Green.

1912), the revivalist preacher often known as 'General' Booth, who in 1865 founded the organisation which became the Salvation Army.

TOTTENHAM

The architect **William Butterfield** (1814-1900) is buried at Tottenham Cemetery, Prospect Place, N17 (west of White Hart Lane station). The coffin tomb, designed by Butterfield for himself and his family, is in medieval style and is topped by a cross. Butterfield's sister lived in Tottenham.

TOWER OF LONDON

In the chapel of St Peter ad Vincula, in the Tower of London, was buried the headless body of **St Thomas More** (1478-1535), Lord Chancellor of England; his head is allegedly in a vault at St Dunstan's church, Canterbury. Other victims of royal displeasure buried at the chapel include **Thomas Cromwell** (1485?-1540), statesman and sometime favourite of Henry VIII; **Edward Seymour** (1506?-52), first Earl of Hertford and Duke of Somerset ('Protector Somerset'); **Catherine Howard** (d.1542), fifth queen of Henry VIII; **Lady Jane Grey** (1537-54), who was proclaimed queen in 1553; and James Scott (1649-85), **Duke of Monmouth and Buccleuch**, natural son of Charles II.

Sir Thomas More

WEST BROMPTON

Brompton Cemetery, Old Brompton Road, SW5, opened in 1840 and is one of the finest of London's cemeteries, containing the tombs of many famous people. Starting from the North Lodge on Old Brompton Road, to find the tomb of **Emmeline Pankhurst** (1858-1928), leader of the militant movement for women's suffrage, cross North Walk and proceed along Central Avenue. The grave, marked by a Celtic cross in brown sandstone, is on the left beside the path after about 100 yards (90 metres). The ledger grave of the tenor **Richard Tauber** (1891-1948) is about 30 yards (27 metres) further along Central Avenue, also just to the left of the path.

Take the first path on the left and the second on the right, and the grave of the

A tall Celtic cross marks the grave of Emmeline Pankhurst (1858-1928) in Brompton Cemetery. The cross is brown marlstone, a soft sandstone from Northamptonshire that contains many fossils. The memorial, listed grade II, bears a relief carving of a draped figure in the manner of Eric Gill.

author **George Henry Borrow** (1803-81) is on the left of the path after about 50 yards (45 metres). Take the next left and follow the path to the East Terrace; on the right is the tomb of **Sir Henry Cole** (1808-82), founder and first director of the South Kensington Museum (later the Victoria and Albert Museum).

Return along the same path but take the second on the left; beside the path and to the left, after about 20 yards (18 metres), is the grave of **John Wisden** (1826-84), the Sussex and England cricketer who founded *Wisden's Cricketers' Almanac*. It has a new and disappointing headstone of dark grey polished granite, showing a cricketer; this was erected on the centenary of his death. Continue along the path, turning right at the massive granite mausoleum designed for Lord Kilmorey (who disliked it and was buried elsewhere). Turn left at Central Avenue; after a short distance, set back on the left is the grave of **George Godwin** (1815-88), architect and editor of *The Builder* from 1844 until 1883. His grave displays a portrait medallion and mourning figures. Take the next left; just before the East Terrace is reached, the tomb on the left surmounted by a lion is that of **'Gentleman' John Jackson** (1769-1845), the boxer who was English champion during 1795-1803, then ran a boxing school in Bond Street. His altar tomb, with a portrait on its side, was originally decorated with figures of athletes, but these have been removed. Walk southward along the terrace, and after about 40 yards (37 metres) the grave of **Sir Samuel Cunard** (1787-1865), the ship-owner who founded the company which became the Cunard Line, is marked by two huge flat slabs of polished granite, the smaller upper one pink, the lower one grey.

Return northward along the terrace, taking the first left and turning left at the first intersection, right at the second. To the right of the path, about half-way towards Central Avenue, is the grave of **George Alfred Henty** (1832-1902), the writer of boys' stories. Continue towards Central Avenue, turning left and passing through the Great Circle. To the right of the path, just as the Avenue leaves the Circle, is the pink granite coffin chest of **Sir George Dashwood Taubman Goldie** (1846-1925), the founder of Nigeria.

Pass around the chapel and continue towards the South Walk; just to the right of the T-junction, on the far side of the Walk, is the tomb containing the ashes of the musician **Constant Lambert** (1905-51). Head north along the South Walk, turning left at the T-junction; after a short distance, the grave just to the left of the path is that of **Sir Francis Pettit Smith** (1808-74), who invented a four-bladed screw propeller in 1836. **Samuel Smiles** (1812-1904), the author and social reformer who published *Self-help* in 1859, is also buried at Brompton Cemetery. The south gate of the cemetery, leading to the Fulham Road, is about 50 yards (45 metres) south-east of Smith's grave.

Joseph Aloysius Hansom (1803-82), architect and inventor of the 'Patent Safety Cab' (1834), was buried at St Thomas's Roman Catholic Cemetery, Rylston Road, SW6.

WEST HAM
The ashes of the London-born theatre manager **Lilian Mary Baylis** (1874-1937), who died in Stockwell, were scattered at the East London Cemetery, Grange Road, West Ham, E13.

WESTMINSTER
The body of **Sir Walter Ralegh** (1552?-1618), naval commander, is buried before the altar of St Margaret's church, Westminster, which stands in Parliament Square. A memorial in its original stone surround with Ralegh's 'lightning'

Sir Walter Ralegh

shield is on the wall south of the chancel. After Ralegh's execution his wife removed his head, keeping it with her until her death; it is said it was eventually buried at West Horsley in Surrey, although another opinion holds that it was brought to St Margaret's and interred next to Ralegh's remains. Interred in the churchyard of St Margaret are many notables including **William Caxton** (1422?-91), the first English printer, who established a press at Westminster in 1477, and **John Cleland** (1709-89), the novelist who published *Fanny Hill* in 1750. As the churchyard was cleared for the erection of stands during Queen Victoria's jubilee, the sites of the graves are lost.

   Cardinal Nicholas Patrick Stephen Wiseman (1802-65), who became Cardinal Archbishop of Westminster in 1850, was initially interred at St Mary's Roman Catholic Cemetery, Harrow Road, Kensal Green, NW10. In 1907 his body, and a monument designed by E. W. Pugin, were transferred to Westminster Cathedral. It is in the crypt, which is not normally open to visitors. However, the grave of **Cardinal John Carmel Heenan** (1905-75) is in the floor of the nave, west of the pillar which supports the pulpit.

Westminster Abbey

There are a vast number of graves in Westminster Abbey (usually marked by inscribed stones in the floor), and also many monuments to those whose graves are elsewhere, both in the abbey and at completely different locations. The graves described here may be found by entering the abbey through its west door and progressing up the north aisle of the nave, clockwise around the ambulatory and its chapels, and back via the cloisters and the south aisle of the nave to St George's Chapel and finally the west door.

NORTH AISLE AND CENTRE OF NAVE

Enter through the west door. Immediately ahead is the grave of the **'Unknown Warrior'**. The remains of an unknown soldier from a First World War battlefield were buried here on 11th November 1920, 'to lie among the most illustrious of the land'. To start your tour of these, cross the west end of the nave, passing under the north-west belfry tower, and walk up the north aisle. Immediately to the left are stones covering the ashes of **Clement Richard Attlee** (1883-1967), first Earl Attlee, prime minister 1945-51, and the husband and wife social reformers **(Martha) Beatrice Webb** (1858-1943) and **Sidney James Webb** (1859-1947), Baron Passfield, who was also an historian. (Stones to Ernest Bevin and Ramsay Macdonald are memorials only.) In the next bay but one, low down on the wall under the Parsons Window, is a stone with the famous epitaph 'O rare Ben Johnson'. **Benjamin 'Ben' Jonson** (1573?-1637), poet and dramatist, who was probably born in Westminster, is buried here. Close to it is a brass showing an inscription beneath a canopy; this is the grave of **John Hunter** (1728-93), the surgeon and anatomist, whose body was moved from the vaults of St Martin's to Westminster Abbey by the College of Surgeons.

   Slightly further east, and in the centre of the nave, is the grave of **David Livingstone** (1813-73), the missionary and explorer; his body was interred in the abbey eleven months after his death in Africa. Nearby, in the centre of the aisle, is a metal gravestone dating from 1974 which marks the resting place of the engineer **Thomas Telford** (1757-1834). The civil engineer **Robert Stephenson** (1803-59) was buried next to Telford's grave at his own request; his brass shows an effigy in contemporary dress. Just to the east, two fine Victorian brasses mark the graves of the architects **Sir Charles Barry** (1795-1860), who built the Houses of Parliament, and **Sir George Gilbert Scott** (1811-78).

   Just south of the nave altar are buried the ashes of two prime ministers: **Andrew Bonar Law** (1858-1923), prime minister 1922-3; and **(Arthur) Neville Chamberlain** (1869-1940), prime minister 1937-40. East of the altar is the grave of **Sir**

Joseph John Thomson (1856-1940), the physicist who discovered X-rays in 1895; nearby are those of the physicist **Ernest Rutherford** (1871-1937), Baron Rutherford of Nelson, and **William Thomson** (1824-1907), Baron Kelvin, the scientist and inventor who formulated the laws of thermodynamics.

Through the ticket booth, the splendid monument standing against the choir screen, just to the north of the entrance to the choir, commemorates the resting place of the natural philosopher **Sir Isaac Newton** (1642-1727). Close by in the north aisle is the grave of the astronomer **Sir John Frederick William Herschel** (1792-1871), first baronet, and beside him is the grave of the naturalist **Charles Robert Darwin** (1808-82).

Advance into the north choir aisle, where stones cover the ashes of the composers **Ralph Vaughan Williams** (1872-1958) and **Herbert Howells** (1892-1983). (Those to Elgar, Stanford and Walton are memorials only.) A little further east is the grave of the composer **Henry Purcell** (1658?-95), once the abbey's organist. He was buried in this aisle as the organ once stood above it. Nearby is the grave of **William Sterndale Bennett** (1816-75), composer and principal of the Royal Academy of Music.

NORTH TRANSEPT

Continue past the west aisle of the north transept and turn left towards the north door, at the end of the transept. A standing figure wearing the robes of the Order of the Garter marks the grave of Henry John Temple (1784-1865), third **Viscount Palmerston**, who was prime minister during 1855-8 and 1859-65. Next to him is the elaborate monument to **William Pitt 'the Elder'** (1708-78), first Earl of Chatham, who was prime minister during 1766-8. His grave, however, is in the centre of the aisle, under a black slab, the inscription almost worn away. He shares his grave with his son, **William Pitt 'the Younger'** (1759-1806), who was prime minister during 1783-1801 and 1804-6. Just north of the Pitt grave is that of the statesman **Charles James Fox** (1749-1806); at the head of this grave, a plain stone marks the resting place of **Henry Grattan** (1746-1820), the Irish statesman who died in London. Also buried in the centre of the transept, a little to the south, are the philanthropist **William Wilberforce** (1759-1833), the statesman **George Canning** (1770-1827) and, adjacent to the Pitts' grave, Robert Stewart (1769-1822), second Marquis of Londonderry, better known as **Viscount Castlereagh**, who committed suicide at his country seat. Further south is the grave of **William Ewart Gladstone** (1809-98), who was prime minister on four occasions between the 1860s and 1890s; his statue is by the east wall, close to his grave.

SANCTUARY

Turn left into the ambulatory. On the right is the sanctuary or shrine (at the time of writing closed for restoration). The tomb of **Anne of Cleves** (1515-57), the fourth queen of Henry VIII, is immediately to the south; it stands below a tapestry and is topped by a marble slab. On the north side of the sanctuary, just north of the high altar, is the tomb of **Edmund Lancaster** (1245-96), Earl of Lancaster, called Crouchback. Beyond the high altar is the Chapel of Edward the Confessor, centred on the massive shrine of **Edward the Confessor** (c.1003-66), king of the English. The tomb of **Edward I** (1239-1307) stands on the north side of the sanctuary, to the north of the high altar, with the tomb of **Henry III** (1207-72) to its right (although Henry III's heart was sent to Fontevraud). Next is the tomb of **Eleanor of Castile** (c.1245-90), queen of Edward I, while at the east end of the sanctuary is the tomb of **Henry V** (1387-1422). On the south side of the sanctuary are the tombs of **Edward III** (1312-77) and, just south of the high altar, **Richard II** (1367-1400).

CHAPEL OF ST PAUL

Continue east along the north ambulatory and pass the chapel of St John the Baptist

Edward Hyde, Earl of Clarendon.

before entering the next chapel, dedicated to St Paul. In the floor immediately to the left of the gate is the tomb of **Sir Rowland Hill** (1795-1879), instigator of the penny post. Leave the chapel and turn left, coming at once upon the tomb of Edward Hyde (1609-74), first **Earl of Clarendon**, which lies at the foot of the steps leading to Henry VII's Chapel.

HENRY VII'S CHAPEL

At the very east end of the abbey is the magnificent chapel of Henry VII. Begin with the north aisle. At its entrance is the grave of **Joseph Addison** (1672-1719), essayist and Whig MP, and next is the vault containing **George Monck** (1608-70), first Duke of Albemarle, who engineered the restoration of Charles II. Further east is the white marble tomb of **Queen Elizabeth I** (1533-1603); beneath her coffin rests that of her half-sister, **Queen Mary I** (1516-58). A sarcophagus standing against the east wall of the aisle probably contains the bones of **Edward V** (1470-83).

In the centre of the chapel's nave is a plain stone marking the grave of **George II** (1683-1760), who is buried near his queen, **Caroline** (1683-1737). Beyond the altar is the vault containing the tomb of the builder of the chapel, **Henry VII** (1457-1509), and beside him is the tomb of James VI (1566-1625), king of Scotland, afterwards **James I**, king of England. Beneath the altar at the head of Henry VII's tomb is the grave of **Edward VI** (1537-53). In the chapel immediately to the north of the altar is the tomb of **George Villiers** (1592-1628), first Duke of Buckingham, the court favourite who was assassinated at Portsmouth.

The small chapel to the east of the altar, at the easternmost point of the abbey, is the RAF Chapel, dedicated in 1947 to the memory of the men of the Royal Air Force who lost their lives in the Battle of Britain. The 'Father of the Royal Air Force', **Hugh Montague Trenchard** (1873-1956), first Viscount Trenchard, is buried here, as well as **Hugh Caswall Tremenheere Dowding** (1882-1970), first Baron Dowding, who was chief of Fighter Command during the Battle of Britain.

Returning to the the south aisle of Henry VII's Chapel, enter at its west end, where the grave of **Mary, Queen of Scots** (1542-87), is marked by a white marble effigy upon a sarcophagus; just to the west, in the floor, is the tomb of **Prince Rupert** (1619-82). Beneath the east end of the aisle, just before the altar, is a royal vault containing **Charles II** (1630-85), **William III** (1650-1702), **Mary II** (1662-94), queen of England, Scotland and Ireland, **Queen Anne** (1665-1714) and her consort, **Prince George of Denmark** (1653-1708); they have no monuments in the abbey.

CHAPEL OF ST EDMUND

From Henry VII's Chapel, continue west past the Chapel of St Nicholas to the chapel dedicated to St Edmund. The grave of the novelist **Edward George Earle Lytton**

Bulwer-Lytton (1803-73), first Baron Lytton, lies towards its southern side.

POETS' CORNER AND SOUTH TRANSEPT

Return to the south ambulatory and continue left, then turn left into the south transept and Poets' Corner. Almost immediately on the left is a bust marking the grave of the poet **John Dryden** (1631-1700); nearby lies **Francis Beaumont** (1584-1616), the playwright who wrote several works in collaboration with John Fletcher. Progress southward along the transept: the large canopied tomb on the left, erected in 1556, is that of the poet **Geoffrey Chaucer** (1340?-1400). Nearby is a stone covering the ashes of **John Edward Masefield** (1878-1967), Poet Laureate. By Chaucer's tomb are the gravestones of the poets **Robert Browning** (1812-89) and **Alfred Tennyson** (1809-92), first Baron Tennyson. Almost in the south-east corner of the transept is the tomb of the poet **Edmund Spenser** (1552?-99).

A wall and column divide the east and west sections of the transept. Near this column is the grave of **Samuel Johnson** (1709-84), author and lexicographer; a bust was placed on the wall above his grave in 1939. Next to him is the actor **David Garrick** (1717-79). At the south end of the transept is the grave of the poet and dramatist **John Gay** (1685-1732). Adjacent lie the ashes of the actors **Sir Henry Irving** (1838-1905) and **Sir Laurence Kerr Olivier** (1907-89), Baron Olivier. West of Johnson is the dramatist **Richard Brinsley Sheridan** (1751-1816), and next is the grave of the novelist **Charles John Huffam Dickens** (1812-70), adjacent to the resting place of the ashes of the poet and author **Thomas Hardy** (1840-1928), whose heart was buried at Stinsford in Dorset. Next is the grave of the writer **(Joseph) Rudyard Kipling** (1865-1936), who was awarded the Nobel Prize for literature in 1907; he was cremated secretly at Golders Green and his ashes were buried in the abbey.

The actor David Garrick in his role as Hamlet.

High on the west wall of the transept is a statue of the composer **George Frederick Handel** (1685-1759), overlooking his grave next to Dickens. Just to the north is a statue of the essayist Joseph Addison (1672-1719), whose grave is in Henry VII's Chapel; at the foot of this statue is buried **Thomas Babington Macaulay** (1800-59), first Baron Macaulay, the historian who began his *History of England* in 1839. Towards the north end of the west wall are buried the architect **James Wyatt** (1746-1813), Surveyor to Westminster Abbey in 1776, and the antiquary **William Camden** (1551-1623), his effigy clasping a copy of his *Britannia*. Then comes **Gilbert Murray** (1866-1957), the classical scholar. In the centre of the north part of the transept are the graves of the architect **Robert Adam** (1728-92) and the poet **James Macpherson** (1736-96). The geographer **Richard Hakluyt** (1552?-1616) was also probably buried in this area.

CLOISTERS

Leave the south transept and turn immediately left into the east walk of the cloisters, down the ramp, at the foot of which the dramatist **Aphra Behn** (1640-89) is buried. The inscription on her floor stone reads 'Here lies a proof that wit can never be defence against mortality'. Turn right and follow the right-hand wall to the door back into the south aisle.

South aisle

On the wall at the west end of the south aisle, just before the door leading to the Deanery, is a wall monument marking the grave of the dramatist **William Congreve** (1670-1729).

St George's Chapel

Enter St George's Chapel through the arch at the end of the nave. In the chapel lie the ashes of **Edmund Henry Hynman Allenby** (1861-1936), first Viscount Allenby of Megiddo, field marshal.

WHITECHAPEL

The former churchyard of the demolished St Mary Matfelon, Adler Street, is the claimed resting place of **Richard Brandon** (d.1649), the executioner whose victims included Charles I. The site is now Altab Ali Park and there is no memorial.

In the small and crowded Jewish cemetery, Brady Street, E1 (east of Whitechapel underground station), is the grave of **Nathan Meyer Rothschild** (1777-1836), the financier and merchant, who established a branch of his banking business at New Court, St Swithin's Lane, in 1805. He died in Germany and his remains were returned to Brady Street, which is now closed to burials and has limited access.

WILLESDEN

The Jewish United Synagogues Cemetery, Glebe Road, Willesden, NW10, has the highest profile of London's Jewish cemeteries and contains the graves of many important Jewish families. The Rothschild tombs, within the balustraded enclosure west of the main axial path, include those of **Sir Nathan Mayer Rothschild** (1840-1915), second baronet and first Baron Rothschild, banker and philanthropist, the

The grave of Sir Lionel Walter Rothschild (1868-1937), third baronet and second Baron Rothschild, FRS (1911), at the Jewish Cemetery in Willesden. As well as working in the family bank, Rothschild founded the natural history museum at Tring; its collection was eventually bequeathed to the British Museum. The base of his headstone is decorated with floral carvings.

first professing Jew to enter the House of Lords; and **Lionel Nathan de Rothschild** (1808-79), banker and MP for the City of London during 1858-74. Other Rothschild tombs are in enclosures facing the end of the path, and further into the cemetery a hedged enclosure on the west side contains the tomb of **Lionel Walter, Lord Rothschild** (1868-1937), whose private collection now forms the natural history museum in Tring, Hertfordshire. His gravestone is inscribed 'Who teaches us more than the beasts of the earth'. Also here are **Solomon Barnato Joel** (1865-1931), the financier and sportsman, and **Harry (Jim) Joel** (1895-1992), the racehorse owner. The Joel family enclosure, south-west of the Prayer House, displays a combination of pink and grey granite and marble stones, as well as elaborate ironwork. North-west is the art dealer and benefactor **Joseph Duveen** (1869-1939). To the east (left-hand side) of the drive to the Prayer House are the graves of **Sir Charles Clore** (1904-79), financier and industrialist, and **Sir John Edward Cohen** (1898-1979) of Tesco.

WIMBLEDON

The publisher and guide-book writer **John Murray** (1808-92), who lived in Wimbledon for nearly half a century, was buried at the parish church, St Mary, Church Road, SW19.

MIDDLESEX

HESTON

The naturalist and collector **Sir Joseph Banks** (1743-1820) was buried in the church of St Leonard, Heston Road, Heston, close to his home. He was buried in the vault but had stipulated that his grave should be unmarked. After his death his widow allowed a memorial plaque to be placed on the north wall by the Royal Society, of which Banks had been president.

RUISLIP

The ashes of the actress **Jessie Margaret Matthews** (1907-81) were laid in the Garden of Rest at St Martin, High Street, Ruislip.

STANMORE

The ashes of **Sir William Schwenck Gilbert** (1836-1911), the dramatist who collaborated with Sir Arthur Sullivan on a long series of comic operas, were buried in the churchyard of St John the Evangelist, Church Road, Great Stanmore, which was close to his home. His grave, surmounted by a white marble angel, is to the left as you face the south porch.

TEDDINGTON

Richard Doddridge Blackmore (1825-1900), the author of *Lorna Doone* (1869), was buried at Teddington Cemetery, Shacklegate Lane, Teddington. In 1857 an inheritance allowed Blackmore to build a country house at Teddington. He named it Gomer House, after a favourite dog, and moved in during 1860, living there for the last forty years of his life. His dark red polished marble headstone is on the left of the main drive, 50 yards (45 metres) from the entrance to the cemetery.

TWICKENHAM

The poet **Alexander Pope** (1688-1744) is buried in the parish church of St Mary, Church Street, Twickenham. In 1719 Pope leased a villa at Crossdeep in Twickenham. He lived there for the rest of his life, spending much time on improving the gardens. He was buried beside his mother in the centre aisle of the church, by the chancel step, under a small stone incised 'P'. A brass plaque was placed next to it in 1962. In the north gallery are a memorial to Pope's parents (at the east end) and a monument erected to Pope in 1861, a relief of an obelisk with a portrait medallion. Also buried in St Mary's is **Sir Godfrey Kneller** (1646-1723), the portrait painter. He was churchwarden here. There is no memorial except a window in the north aisle depicting his coat of arms. Outside the church, on its north-east corner, are memorials to two other Twickenham residents, **Thomas Twining** (1676-1741), who founded the eponymous tea merchants, and **Kitty Clive** (1710-85), a popular actress.

The stamp dealer **(Edward) Stanley Gibbons** (1840-1913) is buried at Twickenham Cemetery, Hospital Bridge Road, Twickenham. He moved to London in 1874, eventually setting up business in Gower Street. He was married five times, lastly to the daughter of a Kensington wine merchant, but had no children. To find his grave, take the central of three paths from the monkey-puzzle tree by the chapel and walk 90 yards (80 metres). Gibbons has a floral white cross on the right of the drive. Further along, at the corner, is the large rough-hewn granite headstone of **Francis Francis** (1822-86), war correspondent and angler, inscribed 'And angle on and beg to have/A quiet passage to a welcome grave'. He represented *The Times* during the Zulu War and was later fishing editor of *The Field.*

NORFOLK

AYLSHAM

The grave of the landscape gardener **Humphry Repton** (1752-1818) is in the churchyard of St Michael, beside the south wall of the church; the Gothic headstone bears a verse he composed himself. In 1778 Repton had bought a small estate at Sustead, about 6 miles (10 km) north of Aylsham; his brother farmed nearby, while his sister lived at Aylsham, in the house their father had left to his children.

EAST DEREHAM

The poet **William Cowper** (1731-1800) was buried in the church of St Nicholas; in the north transept is a commemorative window depicting Cowper and his pet hares, below which is a memorial with lines by his friend William Hayley, who was also his biographer. Cowper lived in Buckinghamshire with his companion Mary Unwin, until she became ill; in 1795 they stayed briefly with a cousin at Dunham

The memorial window to the poet William Cowper in East Dereham church, though he is more closely associated with Berkhamsted in Hertfordshire and Olney in Buckinghamshire.

Lodge, near Swaffham, before moving to East Dereham. Mary Unwin died in 1796, and Cowper remained in the town until his death.

HOUGHTON HALL

St Martin's church at Houghton Hall contains the Walpole family vault, occupied by, amongst others, **Sir Robert Walpole** (1676-1745), first Earl of Orford. He was the son of an old Norfolk family, prime minister in 1721-42 and built the hall in 1721-5. His youngest son, the author **Horace Walpole** (1717-97), fourth Earl of Orford, was also interred in the vault, although neither has a memorial.

LAMAS

The author **Anna Sewell** (1820-78), who published *Black Beauty* in 1877, was buried in the Quaker burial ground at the meeting house in Lamas. She was born in Great Yarmouth to a Quaker family and from 1867 lived at Old Catton in Norwich with her mother, the poet **Mary Sewell** (1797-1884). Mary Sewell was also buried at Lamas, despite joining the Church of England in 1835. Their headstones are now displayed on the roadside wall of the meeting house in the centre of the village.

Horace Walpole's changes to his home at Strawberry Hill at Twickenham created the fashion for Gothic designs.

LANGHAM

The novelist **Captain Frederick Marryat** (1792-1848), who published *Mr Midshipman Easy* in 1836, is buried in the churchyard of St Andrew and St Mary. He removed from London to settle in Langham in 1843. His house on the Cockthorpe road was demolished in the 1880s. There is a memorial to Marryat in the church, on the north wall of the nave, together with details of the signalling code he devised for the Merchant Navy. His grave is under a pedestal monument close to the south-west corner of the church.

LUDHAM

The ashes of the landscape artist **Edward Brian Seago** (1910-74) were scattered on the marshes near his home in Ludham. Seago was born in Norwich, and many of his best-known works are Broadland scenes, often featuring Ludham and its surroundings.

NORWICH

The nurse **Edith Cavell** (1865-1915), daughter of a Norfolk rector, became a national martyr when she

Nurse Edith Cavell's modest cross in the graveyard outside Norwich Cathedral. She was executed by firing squad in Belgium, where she aided the resistance movement during the First World War, and her remains were returned to Britain at the end of the war. Her reburial at Norwich followed a funeral service in Westminster Abbey.

TO THE PURE
AND HOLY MEMORY
OF

EDITH CAVELL
WHO GAVE HER LIFE FOR ENGLAND
12TH OCTOBER 1915

HER NAME LIVETH FOR EVERMORE

was arrested and shot by German troops while serving in Belgium during the First World War. Her remains were brought back to England at the end of the war and reinterred outside the south-east transept wall of the cathedral.

The tomb of the landscape painter **John Crome** (1768-1821), who was educated in Norfolk and founded the Norwich School of painting, is in the church of St George, Colegate.

WESTON LONGVILLE
In the floor of the chancel of All Saints' church is a diamond slab marking the grave of **Parson James Woodforde** (1740-1803), rector from 1755 to his death, whose *Diaries* paint a vivid picture of life in his village.

WEST WINCH
In the churchyard, among old headstones a few yards from the east end of the church, is the grave of the designer, author and cartoonist **Sir Osbert Lancaster** (1908-86), whose pocket cartoons appeared on the front page of the *Daily Express* for many years.

NORTHAMPTONSHIRE
GREAT BRINGTON
Diana Frances Spencer, Princess of Wales (1961-97), married Prince Charles, heir to the British throne, in 1981. The couple had two sons but separated in 1992. The Princess, who was renowned for her charitable work, died in a Paris car crash. After a service at Westminster Abbey on 6th September 1997, her body was taken by road to the Spencer family home, Althorp, near the village of Great Brington, about 5 miles (8 km) north-west of Northampton. The coffin was then interred on a small island in the centre of a tranquil ornamental lake known as the Oval, just to the north of Althorp House.

NORTHAMPTON
The grave of the geologist and engineer **William Smith** (1769-1839), the 'Father of English Geology', is at the west end of the church of St Peter. Smith happened to be staying with friends in Northampton when he died suddenly.

WEEDON LOIS
The poet **Dame Edith Louisa Sitwell** (1887-1964) often visited the home of her brother Sacheverell and his wife at Weston, just under a mile (a kilometre) west of Weedon Lois; she felt that she could find security with the family at Weston. She is buried in the extension to St Mary's churchyard, which has been cut out of a meadow on the far side of the road. Her tombstone, standing centrally at its farthest end, is a tapering upright slab carrying a square bronze plaque by Henry Moore. It shows two intertwined hands, of a woman and child, which signify Youth and Age. Beneath the plaque are carved the last four lines of her poem 'The Wind of Early Spring'.

NORTHUMBERLAND
BAMBURGH
The canopied tomb west of the church of St Aidan shelters the tomb of the local heroine **Grace Horsley Darling** (1815-42), although the original figurine now resides inside the church. Darling, the daughter of a lighthouse keeper on the Farne Islands, rescued five people from the wreck of the *Forfarshire* in 1838.

KIRKNEWTON
The Northumbrian social reformer **Josephine Elizabeth Butler** (1828-1906) is buried in the churchyard of St Gregory the Great, on the northern edge of the

Edith Sitwell's unusual headstone at Weedon Lois features a bronze by Henry Moore and the last lines of her poem 'The Wind of Early Spring'. She began to write poetry when a child and published her first volume of verse in 1915; the period of her greatest popularity as a poet was the 1940s, when her work was much concerned with the war.

Cheviots. The grave is marked by a grey stone slab bearing a raised cross, which lies beside the south-west corner of the tower. After her husband's death in 1890, Butler lived in London and abroad, eventually returning in 1902 to Wooler (near Kirknewton), the home of George Grey Butler, her eldest son. She died in Wooler during the cold winter of 1906 and was buried at St Gregory, as many of her ancestors had been. In the south-west corner of the churchyard is the splendid Davison family vault containing the body of **Alexander Davison** (1750-1829), government contractor and friend of Lord Nelson. Davison was born in Northumberland, eventually buying Swarland Park, to the south of Kirknewton, in 1795. He much improved the house and grounds and planted trees representing the position of the fleets in the battle of the Nile. He died in Brighton.

KIRKWHELPINGTON

The engineer and scientist **Sir Charles Algernon Parsons** (1854-1931), whose firm built the sensational experimental steam turbine vessel *Turbinia*, is buried at St Bartholomew. His grave is in the extension to the churchyard, beside a path leading from the church to a stone stile. The graves of Sir Charles and his wife are both marked by tall stone crosses; his grave is on the left. Parsons, who was an apprentice at Sir William Armstrong's Elswick works in Newcastle during 1877-81, founded his own firm at Heaton in 1889. His family home was at Ray, just west of Kirkwhelpington.

MORPETH

In the churchyard of St Mary, Great North Road, just over 100 yards (90 metres)

Three separate monuments mark the grave of the suffragette Emily Wilding Davison (1872-1913) in the churchyard of St Mary, Morpeth. The Davison family memorial, a tall white marble pedestal, stands above two smaller personal memorials on the hillside north of the church.

north-west of the church, is the memorial to the suffragette **Emily Wilding Davison** (1872-1913), who died after throwing herself into the path of the King's horse during the Derby of 1913. She was the second child of Charles Davison, a London businessman, and his second wife and former housekeeper, Margaret Caisley. After the failure of Charles Davison's investments, followed by his death in 1893, Mrs Davison returned to their country home, Winton House in Morpeth, later moving further north to Longhorsley. To find the Davison family grave, enter the churchyard at the lychgate and follow the path on the right by the north side of the church, and continue along as it curves to the north. Take the second path on the left uphill to a tall Gothic spire decorated with angels, which stands at a crossing. The Davison grave, marked by a tall white marble pedestal topped with a cross, is immediately to the north. Emily Davison's epitaph is 'Deeds not words', with the biblical quotation 'Greater love hath no man than this, that a man lay down his life for his friends'.

NEWCASTLE UPON TYNE

The Newcastle architect John Dobson laid out the General Cemetery (now known as Jesmond Cemetery), Jesmond Road, and designed its chapels for the Newcastle General Cemetery Company in 1836; it became popular amongst the prosperous families of nineteenth-century Newcastle. Enter through the splendid gateway on Jesmond Road and follow the main path straight ahead; the third stone along in the first row of graves on the right is that of the novelist **Sid Chaplin** (1916-86). Chaplin was born in County Durham and initially worked in the local pit, drawing inspiration for his books and short stories from his work and life in the mining villages. He settled in Newcastle in 1957. Chaplin's grave is marked by two fossiliferous grey limestone boulders, one mounted above the other. Incised into the rock are a feather and the lines 'The sunshine greeted him/The wind caressed him'. Continue along the main path towards the far gateway, turning right at the disused chapel to walk between the cemetery wall and the gravestones. After about 50 yards

The tomb of the architect John Dobson (1787-1865), his wife and two children, is well hidden in the leafy General Cemetery at Newcastle upon Tyne. The grave of Dobson, who laid out the cemetery and designed its chapels, was originally marked by a fine sandstone cross bearing only his initials. This happily understated monument now lies flat before a less appealing headstone dating from 1905.

(45 metres) turn right between an isolated holly bush and a tall red granite pedimented column. Immediately ahead is another pedimented column marking the Arnison family vault. Directly behind this is the railed grave of the architect **John Dobson** (1787-1865). There is a flowery headstone dating from 1905 and (now lying flat) his original headstone, a cruciform sandstone slab inscribed 'J. D.'.

Richard Grainger (1798-1861), the architect, planner and developer who was the driving force behind the creation of the classical centre of Newcastle (now known as Grainger Town), was buried in the churchyard of St James, Benwell Lane, Benwell. His tomb lies within the Grainger family plot, a T-shaped railed enclosure just west of the tower.

OVINGHAM
The wood-engraver **Thomas Bewick** (1753-1828) was buried in the churchyard of St Mary, immediately west of the tower; his large plain stone slab now stands in the church porch. He was born at the Bewick family home, Cherryburn, a farmhouse just across the river Tyne from Ovingham at Eltringham, and spent much of his childhood there. Bewick's most celebrated work was *A History of British Birds*, which was published in 1797-1804. He died in Gateshead.

ROTHBURY
The inventor and industrialist **Sir William George Armstrong** (1810-1900), Baron Armstrong of Cragside, was born in Newcastle upon Tyne, where he later opened a massive engineering works at Elswick. He bought an estate just east of Rothbury in 1863 and there built his country house, Cragside, transforming the original house and estate in dramatic fashion. He died in 1900, and on the last day of

the nineteenth century his remains were laid beside those of his wife, who had died in 1893, in the extension of All Saints' churchyard in Rothbury, overlooking the river Coquet.

THROCKRINGTON

William Henry Beveridge (1879-1963), first Baron Beveridge, the economist and social reformer, is buried at St Aidan, an isolated church perched high on the Whin Sill with vast moorland views. His grave is in the north-west corner of the churchyard and is the most southerly of a line of five Beveridge family graves, four of them having pointed headstones. A small cross is engraved on his headstone. In 1904 Beveridge met Janet Mair, the wife of his cousin David Mair. Soon after the death of David Mair in 1942, Beveridge and Janet married; as Beveridge put it: 'My lady was married to my friend and cousin and I had to wait for her.' Janet died in 1959, and Beveridge then spent much time with his step-children, especially Elspeth Burn, at her house, Carrycoats Hall, about 3 miles (5 km) west of Throckrington, which he came to regard as his second home.

WHITTINGHAM

The grave of the fashion designer **Jean Muir** (1928-95) lies in the churchyard of St Bartholomew, not far from her Scottish roots and her Northumbrian home of Lorbottle Hall, which is 3 miles (5 km) south-west of Whittingham. Miss Muir, who preferred to be called a dressmaker, was the best fashion designer of her day in Britain, her trademark being the utter simplicity of her clothes. Her grave, on the western edge of the churchyard almost opposite the tower, is marked by an elegant grey slate headstone bearing her married name, Jean Elizabeth Leuckert.

NOTTINGHAMSHIRE

HOLBECK

Lady Ottoline Violet Anne Morrell (1873-1938), artistic hostess and patroness in London and at Garsington Manor, Oxfordshire, is buried in the churchyard of St Winifred; her tombstone is by Eric Gill. Ottoline Morrell was step-sister to the sixth Duke of Portland, whose family seat was Welbeck Abbey, just north-west of Holbeck, one of the estate villages. She went to live at Welbeck as a six-year-old when her half-brother succeeded to the dukedom, and she was educated there by her mother, Baroness Bolsover.

HUCKNALL

The poet **George Gordon Byron** (1788-1824), sixth baron, died in Greece and was buried in the family vault of St Mary Magdalen church at Hucknall (originally Hucknall Torkard). There is a memorial in the chancel. Nearby is the family seat, Newstead Abbey. Byron inherited the abbey in 1798 and lived there from time to time before selling it in 1816. Also buried in the family vault is the mathematician and computer pioneer **Ada, Countess of Lovelace** (1815-52), born Augusta Ada Byron, only daughter of Lord Byron. Ada's mother and father separated five weeks after her birth, and Lady Byron returned, with Ada, to her father's estate at Kirkby Mallory, Leicestershire. Ada married William Lord King, later Earl of Lovelace, in 1835. Ada Lovelace was a friend and colleague of Charles Babbage, inventor of the Analytical Engine, a predecessor of the computer. She is acknowledged to be the world's first computer programmer. Although she is buried at Hucknall, there are monuments to her at Newstead Abbey and in the churchyard at Kirkby Mallory, where there is a large and somewhat decayed Gothic shrine, soon to be restored.

NOTTINGHAM

The funeral of **Tommy Lawton** (1919-96), one of the finest centre forwards ever to have played football for England, took place at Bramcote Cemetery, Coventry

Lane. Lawton was a player with the Notts County club in the late 1940s and early 1950s, returning to manage the team and later to write for the local paper.

OXFORDSHIRE

BLADON
In the churchyard of St Martin, formerly the parish church of Woodstock, lie the graves of **Sir Winston Leonard Spencer Churchill** (1874-1965), prime minister 1940-5 and 1951-5, and his parents **Lord Randolph Henry Spencer Churchill** (1849-95) and **Jennie Jerome** (1854-1921), Lady Randolph Churchill. The Churchills were descendants of John Churchill, first Duke of Marlborough, the brilliant general who was awarded Woodstock Manor and Blenheim Palace by Parliament in 1705.

BURFORD
In the churchyard of St John Baptist is the grave of the novelist and antiquary **John Meade Falkner** (1858-1932), author of *Moonfleet* (1898), who contributed to the restoration of the church, donating stained glass and other furnishings.

CHASTLETON
The grave of the sculptor **Sir Richard Westmacott** (1775-1856) lies in the churchyard of St Mary the Virgin, where his third son was rector. He lies under a flat slab, clearly inscribed, between the north wall of the church and the wall of Chastleton House.

CHOLSEY
The crime writer **Dame Agatha Mary Clarissa Christie** (1890-1976) is buried in the churchyard of St Mary. Her grave is marked by a tall headstone, carved by Nicolette Gray, and twenty-five trees were planted in the churchyard to mark the centenary of her birth in 1990. Cholsey church is just over a mile (2 km) south-east of her house, Winterbrook, outside Wallingford, which Christie and her second husband bought in 1934, and where she remained until her death.

ELSFIELD
The ashes of the author and administrator **John Buchan** (1875-1940), first Baron Tweedsmuir, were buried beneath a fine circular gravestone (recut in 1996) on the rising ground by the east wall of the churchyard at St Thomas of Canterbury. Buchan, who published *The Thirty-nine Steps* in 1915, lived at the Manor House in Elsfield during 1919-35, before his appointment as Governor-General of Canada.

EWELME
The grave of the novelist and playwright **Jerome Klapka Jerome** (1859-1927) lies in the churchyard of St Mary, west of the path from the church to the old rectory. After the success of his *Three Men in a Boat* (1889), Jerome moved to Gould's Grove, a farmhouse a mile (less than a kilometre) south of Ewelme, where he worked in the summerhouse (The Nook). He attended Ewelme church, where his ashes were buried after his sudden death in Northampton.

FINSTOCK
The author and active churchwoman **Barbara Mary Crampton Pym** (1913-80) is buried under a simple round-headed stone in the south-east corner of the churchyard of Holy Trinity. She worked in London at the International African Institute in 1946-74, then retired to a cottage at Finstock, where she lived with her sister and their cats.

IDBURY
In the churchyard of St Nicholas is the grave of **Sir Benjamin Baker** (1840-

The grave of William Morris at Kelmscott; the ridge-shaped stone was designed by the architect Philip Webb, friend and partner of Morris. Webb also designed the 'Morris Cottages' in Kelmscott village, which were built at the expense of Jane Morris in 1902 in memory of her husband. Jane described the last words of William Morris as wishing to rid the world of 'mumbo-jumbo', and, with this in mind, the family ensured that his funeral was far from traditional, with the coffin carried from Lechlade station on a decorated hay wain. Eventually, after her death at Bath, Jane Morris (1839-1914) was buried with her husband at Kelmscott.

1907), the civil engineer who worked on the construction of London's early underground railways and built the Forth Bridge. His large memorial, behind the church, comprises two intersecting arches surmounted by a cross.

KELMSCOTT
William Morris (1834-96), the artist, designer, manufacturer and socialist, is buried at St George. The tomb, designed by Philip Webb, is on the far side of the churchyard, near the fence; it is a ridge-shaped stone on blocks, adapted from a Viking tomb house. From 1871 until his death Morris's country home was Kelmscott Manor House.

NETTLEBED
At St Bartholomew, the graves of the writer and traveller **(Robert) Peter Fleming** (1907-71) and his wife, the actress **Dame Celia Johnson** (1908-82), lie together on the far side

The elegantly carved headstone of the actress Celia Johnson (1908-82) in the churchyard at St Bartholomew, Nettlebed. Beside her grave is that of her husband, the writer and traveller Peter Fleming (1907-71). In the south aisle of the church is a stained glass window in his memory, designed by John Piper and showing a tree with tropical birds.

of the churchyard, directly south of the south porch, and close to the hedge. Fleming's headstone has an epitaph that he wrote himself. The family home in his early years was Braziers Park at Ipsden, about 5 miles (8 km) west of Nettlebed, where his grandparents had their house, Joyce Grove, with its large estate. Fleming eventually came into ownership of the Nettlebed estate, although not Joyce Grove, and in 1938 began to build his own house, Merrimoles, there.

NORTH STOKE

The opera singer **Dame Clara Ellen Butt** (1873-1936) died at North Stoke and was buried in the churchyard of St Mary, west of the tower. One of two white crosses within a kerb reads 'Clara Butt Rumford OBE. With her whole heart she sang songs and loved him that made her'.

NUFFIELD

High on the Ridgeway, in the churchyard of Holy Trinity, are buried the ashes of the industrialist and philanthropist William Richard Morris (1877-1963), **Viscount Nuffield**. His black slate slab is just a few yards north of the west end of the church and is inscribed with his name, dates and a coronet. Morris, who died at Nuffield Place, his home for thirty years, incorporated Morris Motors Ltd in 1919 and founded Nuffield College, Oxford, in 1937.

OXFORD

The philosopher and scientist **Roger Bacon** (1214?-94) lived in Oxford around 1250-7 at the Franciscan House (the site in Paradise Square is now a car park). Bacon left Oxford to work in Paris but is thought to have died in Oxford and been buried in the Franciscan burial ground.

The grave of **Edward Bouverie Pusey** (1800-82), leader of the Oxford Movement and professor of Hebrew at Christ Church, is in the cloister garth of Christ Church Cathedral (which serves both as cathedral and college chapel), where he was canon. His portrait bust is in the south aisle of the chancel.

The Martyrs' Memorial of 1841 in St Giles commemorates the Protestant martyrs **Hugh Latimer** (1485?-1555), Bishop of Worcester, **Nicholas Ridley** (1500?-55), Bishop of London, and **Thomas Cranmer** (1489-1556), Archbishop of Canterbury, who were burnt alive in the ditch outside the city wall following their enforced participation in a discussion at Oxford which held them to be heretics. The exact site is marked by a concrete cross in the surface of Broad Street, near the corner of St Giles, and an inscription on the wall of the Master's Lodgings at Balliol College. Cranmer recanted, thus gaining time, but repudiated his statement and was burnt in his turn.

Sir Thomas Bodley (1545-1613), who endowed the Bodleian Library, is buried in the chapel of Merton College, where he became a Fellow in 1564; his memorial is on the west wall of the ante-chapel.

The grave of the author **Kenneth Grahame** (1859-1932), who was educated in Oxford, is in the rambling churchyard of St Cross in St Cross Road (also known as Holywell Cemetery). Grahame was buried with his son, for whom he wrote *The Wind in the Willows* (1908), and who had died whilst an undergraduate at Oxford. The ashes of the theatre critic **Kenneth Peacock Tynan** (1927-80) were also buried at St Cross; he studied at Magdalen College, Oxford, in 1945-8. Here too are the critic and humanist **Walter Horatio Pater** (1839-94), Fellow of Brasenose College, Oxford, and the organist and composer **Sir John Stainer** (1840-1901), who was professor of music at Oxford University during 1889-99. The location of the graves is shown on a plan in the churchyard.

William Laud (1573-1645), Archbishop of Canterbury, was buried in the chapel of St John's College, of which he became a Fellow in 1593 and President in 1611. He was initially buried at All Hallows in London but was reinterred at St John's in 1663.

The antiquary and biographer **John Aubrey** (1626-97) was buried at St Mary Magdalene church, Cornmarket, amongst other Trinity scholars. He attended Trinity College, Oxford, in 1641-3 and was buried at the church after his sudden death whilst passing through the city. A plaque, erected in the 1960s, is in the south-west corner of the south aisle.

The antiquarian **Thomas Hearne** (1678-1735), who was educated at St Edmund Hall, was buried in the churchyard of St Peter in the East; the church was converted to a library in 1968-70 by St Edmund Hall, and the churchyard is accessible through the college. Hearne's is the low table tomb south-east of the east end of the former church. On the left of the pathway from the college to the church is the restored headstone of **James Sadler** (1753-1828), 'the first English aeronaut', who successfully ascended from Oxford in a balloon in 1784. Sadler made some sixty balloon flights in a long and intensive career.

The critic and novelist **Clive Staples Lewis** (1898-1963), who published the first of the 'Narnia' series for children, *The Lion, The Witch and The Wardrobe*, in 1950, was a Fellow at Magdalen College, Oxford, during 1924-54. His home was The Kilns, Kiln Lane, Headington Quarry; he died there and was buried in the churchyard of Holy Trinity, Trinity Road, Headington Quarry, where his grave is marked by a grey slab with an incised cross, between two pines in the south-west part of the churchyard.

The philosopher **Sir Isaiah Berlin** (1909-97), first president of Wolfson College, Oxford, was buried in Wolvercote Cemetery, which is on the Banbury Road, north of the Oxford ring road. **John Ronald Reuel Tolkien** (1892-1978), Oxford professor and author of *The Lord of the Rings* (1955), was also buried there with his wife in the Roman Catholic section. Signs lead to the grave.

SACRED
To the Memory of
JAMES SADLER
He died March 27th 1828
Aged 75 Years.

THIS STONE WAS RENEWED
BY THE
ROYAL AERONAUTICAL SOCIETY
on the Occasion of the Centenary
of the Death of the Above named
JAMES SADLER
THE FIRST ENGLISH AERONAUT
and subsequently after the
bicentenary in 1984 of his
first flight on 4th October.

PIDDINGTON

Opposite the porch of St Nicholas's church is the low wide headstone of **John Drinkwater** (1882-1937), the poet, who as a boy spent his holidays here. He asked to be buried here.

SUTTON COURTENAY

At All Saints' church is the grave of **Herbert Henry Asquith** (1852-1928), first Earl of Oxford and Asquith, prime minister 1908-16, who lived nearby; his chest tomb stands east of the chancel. Here too is the grave of author Eric Arthur Blair (1903-50), who wrote as **George Orwell**; his tomb is east of the south-east end of the church and has roses growing on it. In Orwell's will, there was an unexpected request for a churchyard burial. Orwell had no prior connection with any church, so his friend David Astor, the newspaper proprietor, found him a plot at All Saints, near the Astor family estate.

The remarkable balloonist James Sadler is commemorated in the city of Oxford, from which he made his first ascent.

In Sutton Courtenay churchyard is the chest tomb of the former prime minister Herbert Asquith (1852-1928) and his wife; they lived in a house by the Thames not far from the church.

SWINBROOK

In the churchyard of St Mary are the graves of three of the six Mitford sisters, daughters of the second Baron Redesdale, whose family home was at Swinbrook. The eldest, the author **Nancy Freeman-Mitford** (1904-73), is buried south-west of the tower, near the grave of **Unity Valkyrie Mitford** (1914-48), while **Pamela Jackson** (née Mitford) (1907-94) is buried north-west of the tower. Nancy Mitford settled in Paris after the Second World War, going so far as to buy a plot in the cemetery at Père Lachaise, so that she need not lie forever under grey, English skies. However, her ashes were eventually brought back to Swinbrook and buried in the graveyard she had known as a child. Unity Mitford fell in love with Hitler, shot herself at the outbreak of war and eventually died from her injuries. The inscription on her gravestone reads 'Say not that the struggle naught availeth'. Pamela Mitford married Derek Jackson, the son of a newspaper magnate, but they were eventually divorced, after which she lived quietly as a dog breeder in the country.

WOODSTOCK

In the vault of the chapel at Blenheim Palace is the tomb of John Churchill (1650-1722), first **Duke of Marlborough**, and his wife Sarah (1660-1744). The duke, whose success as commander of the British and Dutch forces in the War of the Spanish Succession earned him a palatial house at Woodstock, named after his victory at Blenheim in 1704, was originally buried at Westminster Abbey but was reinterred at Blenheim on the death of his wife. A magnificent monument to them and their two young sons dominates the chapel.

This splendidly decorative chest tomb at All Saints, Wroxton, commemorates Sir William Pope (d.1631), builder of nearby Wroxton Abbey, and his wife. The alabaster canopy is supported by black marble columns, while the couple's children kneel at their head and foot.

WROXTON

Inside All Saints' church are several splendid monuments, including one dating from 1800 and showing Britannia with a lion; this commemorates Frederick North (1732-92), second Earl of Guilford, better known as **Lord North**, who was prime minister 1770-82. His country seat, Wroxton Abbey, not far from the church, was built by **Sir William Pope** (d.1631), Earl of Downe. He and his wife Ann have an elaborate canopied tomb chest next to the altar. On the north wall of the chancel is a plaque to **Thomas Coutts** (1735-1822), sole partner of the London banking firm Coutts & Company. He died in London, 'after a life honourable to himself and useful to all who enjoyed his friendship', but his remains were brought to Wroxton.

SHROPSHIRE

BROSELEY

The Quaker ironmaster **Abraham Darby** (1677-1717), who evolved a method of casting ironware in sand, moved his works to Coalbrookdale, just across the Severn from Broseley, in the early eighteenth century. He was one of the group of Friends who in 1706 bought a plot of land at Broseley that subsequently became their Quaker burial ground. Darby died at his home, Madeley Court in Coalbrookdale, and was buried at the Broseley burial ground, although there is no marked grave. The burial ground is at the front of the Broseley Pipe Works Museum.

The Quaker burial ground at Broseley, where Abraham Darby was buried in 1717, although his grave is not marked. Many other members of the Darby family were also buried at Broseley, including Abraham's infant daughter Esther in 1709. His wife Mary moved to Bewdley in Worcestershire after his death, as she had not been allowed use of the new house Abraham had been building in Coalbrookdale. She died a year later and was buried at the Quaker burial ground in Bewdley.

LUDLOW

The ashes of the poet **Alfred Edward Housman** (1859-1936) lie outside the north door of the parish church, St Laurence; there is a commemorative tablet on the outer wall of the church. Housman, who published *A Shropshire Lad* in 1896, loved the countryside around Ludlow and Much Wenlock.

MORETON SAY

Robert Clive (1725-74), Baron Clive, governor of Bengal, was the son of a poor Shropshire squire. After his successes in India, he returned home to become MP for Shrewsbury in 1760-74. He is buried beneath the floor of St Margaret's church, Moreton Say, about 12 miles (19 km) north-east of Shrewsbury.

SHREWSBURY

The novelist **Mary Gladys Webb** (1881-1927) was born and brought up in Shropshire. After her marriage in 1912, she and her husband became market gardeners, selling their produce in Shrewsbury market, before moving to London in 1921. Her novels, their rustic setting based on the Shropshire landscape, had little success in her lifetime; *Precious Bane* (1924) is her best-known work. She is buried at the Shrewsbury general cemetery, Longden Road, in the older (eastern) section, where there is a fine view of the hills to the south. From the chapel, follow the path nearest the road westward, turning downhill to the left just before a long hedge. The grave, marked by an upright white marble cross, is on the right of this path, opposite the second path off to the left.

In the churchyard of St Chad, on St Chad's Terrace (now a small park), is the gravestone of **'Ebenezer Scrooge'**, the curmudgeonly character in Charles Dickens's novel *A Christmas Carol* (1843). The large, horizontal slab lies at the end of a small path running left of the main walk, nearly 50 yards (45 metres) from the entrance. The name was inscribed on the otherwise anonymous stone when the novel was being filmed in Shrewsbury.

SOMERSET

BATH

In Bath Abbey, under pew 33 of the nave, is the grave of **Richard Nash** (1674-1762), better known as Beau Nash, gambler and 'king of Bath', who moved to Bath in 1705 and transformed it into an important social centre. There is a plaque, with a long Latin inscription, on the wall of the south aisle next to the crossing. Also here is the political economist **Thomas Robert Malthus** (1766-1834), best known for *An Essay on the Principle of Population* (1798), who was buried in the porch of the abbey. His memorial is the first on the left as you enter. In 1804 Malthus married Harriet, the daughter of John Eckersall of Calverton House, St Catherine, just north of Bath. Malthus died suddenly whilst he and his family were spending Christmas at Calverton House.

Lansdown Cemetery in Lansdown Road was created in 1848 from a pleasure ground originally belonging to **William Beckford** (1760-1844), at one time amongst the richest men in England, whose home was Lansdown Crescent. He was a great traveller and the builder of the staggering Gothic folly Fonthill Abbey. He died in Bath in 1844 and was buried in the Abbey Cemetery, although he had expressed a wish to lie beside the Italianate tower he built in 1825-7 on Lansdown Hill, and which was designed by the architect **Henry Edmund Goodridge** (1797-1864). After Beckford's death, his daughter gave the land around the tower to Bath for use as a public cemetery, and Beckford was re-interred there in 1848 in a pink granite chest, which he and Goodridge had designed. The tomb is reached from a green path leading from the gates and stands on a mound surrounded by a ditch. Nearby was the

The polished pink granite chest tomb of the folly builder and wealthy traveller William Beckford in Lansdown Cemetery, Bath, resting on a grassy plinth and separated from other monuments by its own ditch. Beckford's architect, Henry Edmund Goodridge, designed the cemetery's grand Italianate gatehouse, where pedestrians enter through an archway beneath the inscription 'The Gates of Death'.

grave of Beckford's favourite dog, Tiny, now lost. Goodridge's tomb lies to the south of the path.

The author **Frances (Fanny) Burney** (1752-1840), Madame D'Arblay, moved to Bath with her husband, General Alexandre D'Arblay, in 1815. He died there, and Fanny Burney left for London in 1818. The general and their son, who predeceased his mother, are buried with Fanny Burney in a vault in the old burial ground of St Swithin's church, Walcot Street; however, their Portland stone memorial (which dates from 1906) has been moved to the churchyard, so the exact site of the vault is unknown.

BUCKLAND DINHAM

The poet **Sir Henry John Newbolt** (1862-1938), famous for his rousing nautical ballads including 'Drake's Drum' (1897), is buried in the churchyard of St Mary's church, which is located on a small island at the west end of a lake in the grounds of Orchardleigh Park, just over a mile (2 km) east of Buckland Dinham. Orchardleigh Park was the home of the Duckworth family, into which Newbolt married; there is a memorial tablet on the north wall of the church to Newbolt and his wife Margaret (1867-1960). Their graves are at the east end of the churchyard, which overlooks the lake; they are marked by two small plain stones. The church is approached through Orchardleigh Golf Course. A track to the right from the main drive is signed to the church. Also in the churchyard is a monument to Azor, a dog buried in 1796 in the tomb of his master Sir Thomas Champneys, and the inspiration for Newbolt's 'Fidele's Grassy Tomb'.

CLEVEDON

Arthur Henry Hallam (1811-33), the subject of Tennyson's *In Memoriam* (1850), died suddenly in Vienna and was buried at St Andrew's church. Hallam, whose home was Clevedon Court, East Clevedon, met Tennyson whilst studying at Trinity College, Cambridge.

COMBE FLOREY

In the churchyard of St Peter and St Paul is the grave of the novelist **Evelyn Arthur St John Waugh** (1903-66), who lived at the manor house from 1956 until his death.

EAST COKER

The pirate and navigator **William Dampier** (1651-1715) was the son of a tenant farmer from East Coker. Having been brought up in the village, he was sent to sea in 1668, after the death of his mother. He died in London and was buried at St Michael. Here too, inside the church, were buried the ashes of the poet and playwright **Thomas Stearns Eliot** (1888-1965), whose ancestors had lived in the village but left for America in 1669. The second part of his poem *Four Quartets* (1943) is named and concerned with 'East Coker'; two lines from the poem are quoted on Eliot's memorial tablet in the church.

LANGPORT

The economist **Walter Bagehot** (1826-77) was born in Langport, at a house near the Langport Arms, educated at Bristol and entered his father's shipowning and banking business in 1852. He died at Herds Hill, a large house to the west of the town, and was buried at the parish church, All Saints.

MELLS

There are several significant graves at St Andrew, in the area towards the east wall of the churchyard. These include the author **Siegfried Loraine Sassoon** (1886-1967), whose home for many years, until his death there, was Heytesbury House,

The churchyard at St Andrew, Mells. The headstone on the right is that of the writer Siegfried Sassoon, while on the left lies the politician Christopher Hollis. Like these examples, most of the headstones in the churchyard are unobtrusive, although Eric Gill and Sir Edwin Lutyens both designed stones for members of the Horner family, owners of the Mells Park estate, who were buried nearby.

Heytesbury, near Warminster, about 10 miles (16 km) south-east of Mells. It was Sassoon's wish that he should be buried near his mentor, the Roman Catholic priest **Ronald Arbuthnot Knox** (1888-1957), whose grave is also here. Knox, a scholar who gained a wide reputation as a journalist, broadcaster and writer of detective stories, lived for some years at the Manor House in Mells. Close to Sassoon's grave is that of the author and Conservative politician **(Maurice) Christopher Hollis** (1902-77). Mells Park and its estate were owned for many years by the Horner family. There are a number of Horner graves in this part of the churchyard, while inside the church, in the Horner Chapel (north of the chancel), is the family vault and an equestrian bronze by Sir Alfred Munnings commemorating Edward Horner, killed in France in 1917. Raymond Asquith, son of the prime minister Herbert Asquith, married Katherine Horner, who eventually inherited the Mells Park estate. The grave of Raymond Asquith's sister, the political figure **(Helen) Violet Bonham Carter** (1887-1969), Baroness Asquith of Yarnbury, also lies in the east part of the churchyard.

TRULL

The children's writer **Mrs Juliana Horatia Ewing**, née Gatty (1841-85), lived happily in Trull from 1883, when her husband returned from military service overseas. She is buried in the churchyard of All Saints.

WEARE

The comedian Francis Alex Howard (1922-92), who performed as **Frankie Howerd**, is buried in the churchyard of St Gregory.

WRINGTON

The religious writer **Hannah More** (1745-1833) is buried in the churchyard of All Saints; there is a bust in the south porch and a tablet in the church. More was born in Bristol and educated at her sister's boarding school in the city. She lived at Barley Wood, near Wrington, during 1802-28 and started a series of schools in the neighbourhood, before moving to Bristol to spend her last years at Clifton.

STAFFORDSHIRE

BURSLEM
The novelist (Enoch) **Arnold Bennett** (1867-1931) was the son of a solicitor from Hanley, Stoke-on-Trent, and was educated in Burslem, just north of Hanley. He left for London in 1889 and published the first of his novels based on the Potteries, *Anna of the Five Towns*, in 1902. His ashes were interred in his mother's grave at Burslem Cemetery, Hanley Road, Stoke-on-Trent.

DRAYTON BASSETT
Sir Robert Peel (1788-1850), second baronet, prime minister 1834-5 and 1841-6, created the Metropolitan Police or 'Peelers' when Home Secretary in 1829. He was the son of a Lancashire cotton magnate, his wealth enabling him to buy Drayton Manor, just to the north of Drayton Bassett, after which he became MP for nearby Tamworth. His tomb is in the parish church of St Peter.

NEWCHAPEL
The canal engineer **James Brindley** (1716-72) is buried in the churchyard of St James, south of the east wall of the church. He went into business in 1742 at Leek, 6 miles (10 km) east of Newchapel, as a repairer of old machinery.

RANGEMORE
The founder of the brewers Bass & Company of Burton upon Trent was William Bass. His grandson Michael Thomas Bass (1799-1884) considerably expanded the business, which was then taken on by his son, the philanthropist and brewer **Michael Arthur Bass** (1837-1909), first Baron Burton. The Bass family home from 1860 was Rangemore Hall (now a school), 3 miles (5 km) west of Burton. All Saints' church in Rangemore was built by Michael Thomas Bass, although Michael Arthur Bass made substantial additions to the building, including the chancel. Michael Arthur Bass was buried at All Saints; his funeral was attended by fifteen thousand mourners.

STOKE-ON-TRENT
The potter **Josiah Wedgwood** (1730-95) opened his works at Burslem, north of Stoke, in 1759. His potworks at Etruria, the model village he had built just over a mile (2 km) north-west of Stoke, opened in 1769. Wedgwood died at his home, Etruria Hall, and was buried in the churchyard of St Peter ad Vincula, Stoke-on-Trent. There is a portrait medallion of Wedgwood inside the church, which was rebuilt in 1826-9.

Josiah Wedgwood's grave in the churchyard of St Peter ad Vincula in Stoke-on-Trent. The simplicity of his plain, kerbed grave contrasts with his inventiveness in the ceramics industry; he was appointed the Queen's Potter in 1762.

Herbert Minton (1793-1858) entered his father's Stoke-on-Trent ceramics firm at the age of thirteen; he became sole proprietor in 1836 and greatly expanded the pottery manufacturing business. He lived for many years at Hartshill, just north-west of Stoke, where in 1841-2 he built and endowed Holy Trinity church. Minton retired to Torquay in 1855 and died at his home there, Iona, three years later. His body was brought back to Stoke by train and buried in a vault under the chancel floor in Holy Trinity, Hartshill Road, Stoke-on-Trent.

SUFFOLK

ALDEBURGH

At the parish church, St Peter and St Paul, are the graves of the composer (Edward) **Benjamin Britten** (1913-76), Baron Britten; his partner, the tenor **Sir Peter Pears** (1910-86); and his friend and amanuensis, the musician **Imogen Clare Holst** (1907-84). They are grouped together in the lawn cemetery north of the churchyard; Britten and Pears have plain matching blue slate headstones. Britten and Pears settled in Aldeburgh after the Second World War, while Holst moved to Suffolk in 1952 and was artistic director of the Aldeburgh Festival in 1956-7. Also here in the churchyard is the physician Elizabeth Anderson (1836-1917), better known as **Mrs Elizabeth Garrett Anderson**, who is buried in the Garrett family grave, enclosed by low wrought-iron railings, north of the tower.

BOULGE

In the churchyard of St Michael is the grave of the poet and translator **Edward Fitzgerald** (1809-83), best known for his translation of *The Rubáiyát of Omar*

A rose bush, grown from a cutting of one which stood at the tomb of Omar Khayyám in Iran, flourishes beside Edward Fitzgerald's coffin tomb at St Michael in Boulge. The church stands in the grounds of Boulge Hall, the home of Fitzgerald's parents. Fitzgerald, translator of the Rubáiyát, hardly travelled at all but generally led a quiet life in Suffolk, where he sailed and wrote copious letters to his literary friends.

Khayyám, published anonymously in 1859. Fitzgerald was born in Suffolk and lived there for most of his life, including a sixteen-year period when his home was a cottage on his family's estate at Boulge.

BRADFIELD COMBUST
The agriculturalist **Arthur Young** (1741-1820) was born at Bradfield. He was the younger son of the rector and inherited Bradfield Hall in 1785. He is buried with his wife in the churchyard of All Saints in a pedestal tomb on the right as one enters the churchyard. There is a memorial to him in the south aisle of the church.

FRAMLINGHAM
The poet **Henry Howard, Earl of Surrey** (1517?-47), was the son of Thomas Howard, the third Duke of Norfolk, whose family home was Framlingham Castle. Henry Howard was executed for treason in 1547. His elaborate painted alabaster tomb at St Michael was built in 1614; it shows two recumbent effigies and five kneeling children.

LONG MELFORD
The poet **Edmund Charles Blunden** (1896-1974) was emeritus professor at Hong Kong University during 1953-63, returning to live at Hall Mill, Long Melford, from 1965 until his death in 1974. He was buried in the churchyard at Holy Trinity, in the far south-east corner, under a ledger inscribed 'I live still to love still things quiet and unconcerned'.

PLAYFORD
Sir George Biddell Airy (1801-92), Astronomer Royal, is buried in the church-yard of St Mary. His wife, who died in 1841, was the daughter of a Suffolk farmer. Airy resigned the office of Astronomer Royal in 1881 and afterwards lived, with his two daughters, at the White House in Greenwich and at Playford, where he had bought a cottage in 1845. He died at the White House. Their railed graves by the

The railed grave of Thomas Clarkson (1760-1846), philanthropist and abolitionist, and his family in the churchyard of St Mary, Playford; the Astronomer Royal, Sir George Biddell Airy, was also buried here. A granite obelisk, erected in 1857 in memory of Clarkson, 'the Friend of Slaves', dominates the churchyard, while inside the church are busts of Clarkson and Airy.

101

chancel door are next to those of **Thomas Clarkson** (1760-1846) and his family. Clarkson, the abolitionist, lived at Playford Hall for thirty years. The churchyard is dominated by an obelisk to his memory, inscribed 'The friend of slaves'.

THORNHAM PARVA
The architect **Sir Basil Urwin Spence** (1907-76) died at his home in Eye and was buried in the churchyard (the south-east section) of St Mary at Thornham Parva, a village about 2 miles (3 km) to the west.

SURREY

BROOKWOOD
Brookwood Cemetery, just west of Woking, was opened in 1854 by the London Necropolis and National Mausoleum Company and is the largest cemetery in the United Kingdom. It was served by special funeral trains bringing coffins for burial, until its London terminus was bombed in 1941; the remains of the platforms of the cemetery stations can still be found in the grounds, off Long Avenue and at the end of St Cyprian's Avenue. Maps of the cemetery are located beside the entrances to the grounds off Cemetery Pales, the road which bisects it. The Brookwood Cemetery Society conducts guided walks throughout the year (write to 37 Victoria Road, Knaphill, Woking, Surrey GU21 2AH for details).

Amongst the huge number of people buried here is **Margaret, Duchess of Argyll** (1912-93), the society beauty immortalised in Cole Porter's hit 'You're the Top'. She lies with her first husband, Charles Sweeney, in plot 119 near the former Catholic chapel and has a plain slate headstone. The grave of **Alfred Bestall** (1892-1985), for thirty years the illustrator of the *Rupert Bear* stories, is in plot 100 off Chapel Avenue and is marked by a Celtic cross of grey granite. The social reformer **Charles Bradlaugh** (1833-91) is in plot 108 off Holly Avenue; his memorial, a pink granite pedestal, is surrounded by a yew hedge. The relics of **St Edward the Martyr** (*c*.959-978/9), king of the English, lie in the Orthodox church at the end of St Cyprian's Avenue (signposted from the cemetery entrance); the church is dedicated to St Edward.

The white marble coffin tomb in plot 124, adjacent to the former Catholic chapel, is the grave of the dance-band leader **Carroll Gibbons** (1903-54). The anatomist **Robert Knox** (1791-1862), a good customer of the 'resurrectionists' Burke and Hare, lies in plot 100 off Eastern Avenue; his memorial is a flat stone set well back from the path. The artists and designers **William Frend De Morgan** (1839-1917) and his wife **Evelyn De Morgan** (1855-1919) lie together in plot 24 off St George's Avenue; Evelyn De Morgan designed the headstone with its distinctive pair of figures.

One of Brookwood's most important memorials is that of **Lord Edward Pelham-Clinton** (1836-1907), Master of the Household to Queen Victoria during 1894-1901. His grave, in plot 4 adjacent to St Cyprian's Avenue, is marked by a splendid sculpture group. A modest headstone in the middle of plot 35 ('the Ring') is that of the painter **John Singer Sargent** (1856-1925). A flat grey granite stone some way from Eastern Avenue on the isolated plot 117 marks the grave of **Edith Thompson** (1893-1923) and three other women executed at Holloway Prison. Thompson was hanged because her lover murdered her husband. The author and journalist **Dame Rebecca West** (1892-1983), born Cicily Isabel Fairfield, was buried at Brookwood, in plot 81 off St Andrew's Avenue; she has a plain headstone with no kerb. Also buried here was **Frederick Robert Spofforth** (1853-1926), the Australian cricketer known as 'the Demon Bowler'. The ashes of the author **Dennis Yates Wheatley** (1897-1977) lie in the Glades of Remembrance; his unobtrusive pink granite tablet is near the entrance to the Glades.

Here too, initially, was the grave of the conductor Sir Thomas Beecham (1879-1961), but his body was exhumed in 1991 by his widow and moved to Limpsfield

Above left: *Sheltered by pines at Brookwood Cemetery is this elaborate memorial to Lord Edward Pelham-Clinton.*

Above right: *In contrast, down the road from Brookwood at Pirbright is the rough granite headstone of the explorer H. M. Stanley dominating the churchyard.*

churchyard, where the composer Frederick Delius was buried. Beecham had been a strong champion of Delius's music.

Another exhumation was that of Dodi Fayed (1955-97), the friend of Diana, Princess of Wales; they were both killed in a Paris car crash. Dodi Fayed's body was buried in plot 1 for forty days, then moved by his father, Mohamed Al Fayed, to the family estate at Oxted in Surrey, where a mausoleum is to be built in his memory.

St John's

The village of St John's, which lies on the western edge of Woking about 2 miles from Brookwood Cemetery, is the site of Britain's first crematorium. On 26th March 1885 the first legal human cremation in modern times, that of Mrs Jeannette Caroline Pickersgill of Clarence Gate, London, took place there. The main buildings on the crematorium site date from 1889 and were designed by E. F. Clarke; the chapel is one of the few Victorian crematorium chapels in Britain.

Many cremations have taken place at St John's since 1885, including that of the leader of the theosophists, **Madame Helena Petrovna Blavatsky** (1831-91). Thomas John Barnardo (1845-1905), founder of Barnardo's Homes, was cremated at St John's but buried near the Village Home at Barkingside in Essex. Sir Isaac Pitman (1813-97), inventor of phonography (a type of shorthand), was also cremated at St John's , but his ashes are kept at Golders Green Crematorium in London.

Other cremations include those of Arthur William Patrick Albert (1850-1942), **Duke of Connaught and Strathearn**, third (and last surviving) son of Queen Victoria; the journalist and broadcaster **Richard Frederick Dimbleby** (1913-65);

and **Eadweard Muybridge** (1830-1904), whose work
on animal locomotion led to the invention of cinema-
tography. There is a small memorial over
Muybridge's ashes in the burial area immediately
behind the crematorium.

BURSTOW

The first Astronomer Royal, **John
Flamsteed** (1646-1719), was buried in the
chancel of St Bartholomew. Flamsteed was or-
dained and appointed Astronomer Royal in
1675; he was presented with the living of
Burstow by Lord North in 1684.

BUSBRIDGE

Gertrude Jekyll (1843-1932), garden designer and writer, is buried in the churchyard
at Busbridge, Godalming, in a tomb designed
by her friend and collaborator, the architect
Sir Edwin Lutyens. When Jekyll's father died
in 1876, the family moved to Munstead House,
near Godalming. On an adjoining plot Jekyll

*Gertrude Jekyll, sketched by
her friend Sir Edwin Lutyens.*

began to create a garden and eventually built her own house, Munstead Wood
(designed by Lutyens), during 1893-7. She died at Munstead Wood, having designed over three hundred gardens during her lifetime.

BYFLEET

The publisher **George Smith** (1824-1901), who founded the *Dictionary of National Biography* in 1882, was buried in St Mary's churchyard. After an operation in
early 1901, he left his London home to convalesce at a house he had rented for a few
months in St George's Hill, on the southern edge of Weybridge, close to Byfleet. He

died there shortly afterwards. His grave
is marked by a tall, decorated cross to
the right of the path leading from the
south door to the churchyard.

COMPTON

The painter and sculptor **George
Frederic Watts** (1817-1904) and his
wife Mary lived at Compton from
1891, in a country house called

*The tomb of the eminent Victorian painter
G. F. Watts in front of the cloisters at the
Watts Memorial Chapel in Compton. The
mortuary chapel was designed and built
by his wife Mary with the assistance of a
local builder by the name of Clarence
Sex and several enthusiastic villagers.
Its vaguely Byzantine exterior hides a
complete Art Nouveau interior, one of
the best in Britain, which is weighed down
with symbolic meaning. The Compton
Pottery, initiated by Mary Watts to
provide terracotta work for the chapel,
functioned until 1952.*

Limnerslease, built for them by the architect Sir Ernest George. In 1895, when Compton Parish Council needed a new burial ground, the site chosen was close to their house. Mary Watts undertook to provide a mortuary chapel, which she designed and helped to build; it was completed in 1901. Externally, the chapel is a wonderful mixture of styles, while the interior is completely Art Nouveau, and the whole is in effect a memorial to G. F. Watts. The graves of Watts and his wife, who died in 1938, are up the hill beyond the chapel, in front of the cloisters. The ashes of the writer **Aldous Leonard Huxley** (1894-1963), who published *Brave New World* in 1932, were also buried at the Compton cemetery. Huxley settled in California in 1937 and died there in 1963; his ashes were brought back to Compton and interred in his parents' grave in 1971. It lies to the right of the path from the chapel to the cloisters, surrounded by a carved wooden kerb.

DORKING

The novelist and poet **George Meredith** (1828-1909) lived in Esher from 1859, enjoying long walks in the Surrey countryside. He and his second wife moved to Flint Cottage in Mickleham, 2 miles (3 km) north of Dorking, in 1867. He worked there in a small garden building furnished as a study bedroom, producing one of his most popular novels, *Diana of the Crossways*, in 1885. He died at Flint Cottage and was buried at Dorking Cemetery. His grave, marked with an open book, is in a set of four kerbs, reached by turning right through the entrance gate and left after ten paces.

FARNHAM

The writer and agriculturalist **William Cobbett** (1763-1835) was the son of a Farnham labourer. He published *Rural Rides* in 1830 and farmed at Normandy Farm, 7 miles (11 km) north-east of Farnham, from 1831 until his death there in 1835. He was buried beside his father in the churchyard of St Andrew, Farnham, facing the north porch; there is a medallion bust in the north aisle.

GUILDFORD

The family home of the author and mathematician Charles Lutwidge Dodgson (1832-98), who as **Lewis Carroll** wrote *Alice's Adventures in Wonderland* (1865)

William Cobbett's splendid railed tomb at the church of St Andrew, Farnham, the town of his birth. Cobbett was born in the Jolly Farmer, an inn on Bridge Square, which is now known as the William Cobbett. He began writing and publishing 'Cobbett's Weekly Political Register' in 1802 and continued it until his death in 1835.

105

and *Through the Looking Glass and What Alice Found There* (1871), was The Chestnuts, a large house in Castle Hill, Guildford. He often stayed there, always attending St Mary's church, and occasionally preaching there. He died in Guildford and was buried in the town's Mount Cemetery; his grave, under a pine tree next to the chapel, is marked by a marble cross. The writer and social reformer **Edward Carpenter** (1844-1929), who moved to Guildford in 1922, was also buried at the Mount, in the upper section. The Carroll and Carpenter graves are both clearly signposted. The actor **Boris Karloff** (1887-1969), born William Henry Pratt, was cremated in Guildford and his ashes were buried in the garden of remembrance.

KEW

The co-founder and director of Kew Gardens, the botanist **Sir William Jackson Hooker** (1785-1865), and his son, the botanist and traveller **Sir Joseph Dalton Hooker** (1817-1911), who succeeded his father as director at Kew, were both buried at St Anne, Kew Green. Inside the church are monuments to both men, decorated with ceramic panels of plants. Joseph Hooker was offered a Westminster Abbey burial but chose Kew, the scene of his labours. The artist **Thomas Gainsborough** (1727-88) settled in London at Schomberg House, Pall Mall, in 1774 and was buried in the churchyard of St Anne, by the south wall of the church. By the east end of the church is the tomb of the portrait painter **John Zoffany** (1733-1810), who came to England in 1758.

LALEHAM

The poet and literary critic **Matthew Arnold** (1822-88) was born in Laleham and from 1873 until his death lived at Cobham, 6 miles (10 km) to the south-east. He worshipped in All Saints' church at Laleham and is buried in its churchyard, with other members of his family; there is a brass tablet in the church.

LEATHERHEAD

The novelist Sir Anthony Hope Hawkins (1863-1933), who wrote as **Anthony Hope**, published *The Prisoner of Zenda* in 1894. He lived in London until 1917 but then

The floral grave of the poet Matthew Arnold at All Saints' churchyard in the village of Laleham, his birthplace (although the house where he was born has been demolished, as has his final home, Pain's Hill Cottage at nearby Cobham). He died at Liverpool, awaiting the arrival of his daughter from America.

moved to Heath Farm, Deans Lane, Walton on the Hill, 4 miles (6 km) south-east of Leatherhead, where he died. He was buried in the parish churchyard of St Mary and St Nicholas, Leatherhead, in the white marble family tomb, by the northern entrance from Highlands Road.

LIMPSFIELD

The composer **Frederick Delius** (1862-1934) lived at Grez-sur-Loing, near Fontainebleau in France, from 1897 until his death. He was buried temporarily in the local churchyard, but he had wished to be buried in the south of England. His wife Jelka seached for a suitable churchyard, and in May 1935 his body was brought to England and reinterred with a grey slate headstone in the churchyard of St Peter at Limpsfield; **Sir Thomas Beecham** (1879-1961), the great conductor and an ardent champion of the music of Delius, read the funeral oration and conducted an orchestra playing works by Delius. Beecham was originally buried at Brookwood Cemetery near Woking, but in 1991 his body was transferred to Limpsfield churchyard, close to Delius. His grave faces the roadside bank and is flanked by those of **Norman del Mar** (1919-94), the conductor, and **Eileen Joyce** (1912-91), the Australian-born concert pianist, who lived in the village. Also in the churchyard is the grave of the Harrison sisters, all musicians. **Beatrice Harrison** (d.1965), the cellist, made the first BBC outside broadcast – of the cello and a nightingale.

PIRBRIGHT

The explorer and journalist **Sir Henry Morton Stanley** (1841-1904), born John Rowlands, who met Livingstone in Africa in 1871, died in London and was buried in St Michael's churchyard. His massive monolithic granite headstone bears the epitaph 'Africa'.

RICHMOND

The poet **James Thomson** (1700-48) was educated in Edinburgh; encouraged

In a churchyard full of musicians, at Limpsfield, this headstone is the most evocative. The Harrison sisters rest under a quotation from an ode by Arthur O'Shaughnessy which Elgar set to music.

107

by his friend, the poet David Mallet, he came to London in 1725. Thomson, Mallet and Thomas Arne collaborated on the masque *Alfred*, which was performed in 1740; it contained the song 'Rule, Britannia', for which Thomson probably wrote the words. Thomson, a lover of idleness, lived at Kew Foot Lane in Richmond from 1736 until his death, which resulted from catching a chill on a river trip. He was buried near the front of Richmond parish church, St Mary Magdalene in Paradise Road, although the exact location of his tomb is unknown.

The actor **Edmund Kean** (1787-1833) died in Richmond and was buried in the churchyard of St Matthias, Friars Stile Road; the church was rebuilt in 1858.

SHEPPERTON

The poet and satirist **Thomas Love Peacock** (1785-1866) was the son of a London merchant and worked for the East India Company during 1819-56. He published *Headlong Hall* in 1816. Peacock bought a riverside house for his mother in Lower Halliford, now part of Shepperton, in 1823. He spent many weekends and holidays there. He bought the adjoining property and converted the two into a single house, moving there permanently on his retirement in 1856. He died in 1866 and was buried in the New Cemetery, at the end of the very narrow Cemetery Lane, across the road from Church Square. Turn right at the entrance and take the green path. Peacock's is the last ledger on the right, clearly inscribed. A headstone to his two-year-old daughter, with verses by Peacock, stands by the north wall of the parish church.

WEST HORSLEY

The head of **Sir Walter Ralegh** (1552?-1618), naval commander, is said to lie beneath the south or St Nicholas's chapel of the parish church of St Mary; his body is interred in St Margaret's church in Parliament Square, Westminster. After Ralegh's execution his wife removed the head, keeping it with her until her death; it was eventually buried with his son Carew and two grandchildren at West Horsley, although another version holds that it was returned to St Margaret's. There is no memorial.

WOTTON

The diarist and gardener **John Evelyn** (1620-1706) was born at Wotton House, Wotton, and lived there from 1694. He kept a diary (first published in 1818) from 1641 until his death in London and was buried in the family's mausoleum, to the north of the north chapel in St John's church. There are two plain, coffin-shaped stone slabs commemorating Evelyn and his wife, who died in 1709.

SUSSEX, EAST

BRIGHTON

The poet and diabolist **Edward Alexander 'Aleister' Crowley** (1875-1947) was cremated at Brighton, but the fate of the urn containing his ashes is unknown. It was stolen from its burial place in the garden of a fellow-member of the Order of the Golden Dawn, a group of theosophists involved with black magic.

FLETCHING

The historian **Edward Gibbon** (1737-94) published the first volume of his *Decline and Fall of the Roman Empire* in 1776. He made the acquaintance of the future Lord Sheffield in Lausanne, and when Sheffield's wife died in 1793 Gibbon visited him at his home at Sheffield Park near Fletching. Gibbon stayed several months at Sheffield Park, then returned to London, where he died suddenly. Sheffield had Gibbon's body interred in the family mausoleum, which was an addition to the north transept of St Mary and St Andrew.

FOLKINGTON

The eminent cookery writer and historian **Elizabeth David** (1913-92) spent some of her early years in Eastbourne, just south of Folkington. She died in London, where she had lived for many years. Her funeral at Folkington was followed by a memorial banquet at Wooton Manor, the family home, attended by forty of her friends and based on her favourite recipes. Her slate headstone, in the south-west corner of the churchyard, features a casserole and vegetables.

HOVE

The cricketer **Sir John Berry ('Jack') Hobbs** (1882-1963) is buried at Hove Cemetery, Old Shoreham Road, in the south section. Follow the main drive from the entrance up towards the chapel. Hobbs's is one of the five graves with low headstones and kerbs in white marble on the right, 100 yards (90 metres) before the chapel.

RIPE

The author (Clarence) **Malcolm Lowry** (1909-57), who spent the last eighteen months of his life in Ripe at White Cottage, was buried in the churchyard of St John Baptist. His grave, with small, simple headstone, is to the left as you enter the churchyard.

RODMELL

The writer (Adeline) **Virginia Woolf** (1882-1941) and her husband bought Monk's House, Rodmell, in 1919. The house had a large garden and a view across the river Ouse, in which Woolf drowned herself in 1941; her ashes were buried in the garden.

ROTTINGDEAN

The artist **Sir Edward Coley Burne-Jones** (1833-98), whose home from 1880 was North End House in Rottingdean, was buried with his wife in the churchyard of St Margaret (for which he designed several stained glass windows). There are

In Rottingdean churchyard are the graves of the artist Sir Edward Burne-Jones and the novelists Angela Thirkell and Enid Bagnold.

memorial plaques to them on the church wall, and their grave is just outside the south transept. Beside them, marked by a wooden graveboard, is the grave of their granddaughter, the comic novelist **Angela Margaret Thirkell** (1890-1961), who published *The Brandons* in 1939. She was the mother of the novelist Colin MacInnes, although there was little love lost between them; indeed, in his mother's obituary he described her as 'an immensely successful and bad writer'. The novelist and playwright **Enid Algerine Bagnold** (1889-1981), Lady Jones, who published *National Velvet* in 1935, is also buried here, in the south-east section of the churchyard, beneath one of two ledgers in plain kerbing by a flint wall. In the extension of the graveyard, through the wall south of the tower, a headstone carved with theatre drapes proclaims 'The last curtain call for **G. H. Elliot**, "the Chocolate Coloured Coon", died 1962'. Elliot was a popular music-hall and radio entertainer. The grave is on the right in the middle row.

RYE

The prolific writer **Edward Frederic Benson** (1867-1940) is best known for his 'Lucia' series of social satires, which began with the publication of *Queen Lucia* in 1920. E. F. Benson first visited the author Henry James, a family friend, at Lamb House, West Street, Rye, during 1900; he later stayed at Leasam, just north of Rye, with his friend Lady Maud Warrender. James died in 1916 and Lamb House was eventually and briefly let to E. F. Benson and an artist friend. Benson took up the tenancy permanently in 1919, sharing with his brother, the writer Arthur Christopher Benson (1862-1925), who lived at Lamb House when not in residence at Magdalene College, Cambridge, where he was Master 1915-25. E. F. Benson was Mayor of Rye in 1934-7 and remained at Lamb House until his death in 1940. He was buried at Playden Cemetery, just outside Rye.

WEST FIRLE

The artists and fellow Bloomsbury Group members **Duncan James Corrowr Grant** (1885-1978) and **Vanessa Bell** (1879-1961), who lived together until Bell's death, are buried side by side by the north wall of the churchyard of St Peter. Charleston, the Bloomsbury Group's country house where both Bell and Grant lived for a time, is 2 miles (3 km) east of West Firle.

WITHYHAM

The writer and gardener **Victoria Mary ('Vita') Sackville-West** (1892-1962) was born and brought up at Knole, the family seat in Kent. She and her husband Harold Nicolson bought Sissinghurst Castle, Kent, in 1930, restored the mansion and created a beautiful garden. After her death at Sissinghurst, her ashes, contained in the small pink marble sarcophagus which had held her inkwells, were buried in the parish church of St Michael, Withyham, near the former home of the Sackvilles. A fine slate plaque marks their resting place in the Sackville Chapel.

SUSSEX, WEST

BURPHAM

The author **Mervyn Laurence Peake** (1911-68) is buried in the churchyard of St Mary, where his parents were buried; he lived in the village from time to time between 1938 and 1944. His is among the post-war graves, north of the church.

BURY

The playwright and novelist **John Galsworthy** (1867-1933), author of *The Forsyte Saga* (1922), bought a country home, Bury House, in Bury in 1920. He then spent much of his time in the village; the house had views of the Bury Hill area of the South Downs, where he used to ride. After his death at his Hampstead home, his ashes were scattered on Bury Hill.

CHICHESTER

The ashes of the composer **Gustav Theodore Holst** (1874-1934) were buried in the north transept of Chichester Cathedral, close to the memorial to the composer Thomas Weelkes, whose music Holst loved. (Weelkes was the cathedral's organist around 1608 and was buried at St Bride's, London.)

CRAWLEY

Lord Alfred Bruce Douglas (1870-1945), best known for his intimacy with Oscar Wilde, was buried in the graveyard of the Franciscan Friary; he became a Roman Catholic in 1911. His grave is beside that of his mother, who supported him after his allowance was cut off by his father during his friendship with Wilde. To find his grave, turn right on entering by the graveyard gates and follow this path to its far end (behind the church of St Francis), where the grave is marked by a flat stone.

HORSTED KEYNES

Harold Macmillan (1894-1986), first Earl of Stockton, prime minister 1957-63, is buried in the family plot (surrounded by a hedge) at St Giles's church.

IFIELD

Mark Lemon (1809-70) was the co-founder and first editor of *Punch*; he edited the magazine from 1841 to 1870. He lived in Vine Cottage, Ifield (now part of Crawley), from 1858 until his death in 1870 and attended St Margaret, Ifield, where he was buried in the churchyard. His grave lies south-east of the church and has inscribed stone kerbing.

Mark Lemon

SOUTHWATER

In 1895 the poet **Wilfrid Scawen Blunt** (1840-1922) moved to Newbuildings Place in Southwater, which had been in his family since 1757. Blunt, who kept a stud farm, was buried at Southwater, in the ride through the woods behind the house. The grave is a large grassy mound amongst a row of yew trees that Blunt planted under the oaks.

WEST GRINSTEAD

The writer **(Joseph) Hilaire (Pierre René) Belloc** (1870-1953) was buried in the Catholic churchyard of Our Lady and St Francis with his wife and son. Since 1906 Belloc had lived in the house called King's Land at Shipley, 2 miles (3 km) north-west of West Grinstead, and he died there.

WORTHING

Broadwater Cemetery, 2 miles (3 km) north-east of Worthing, contains the graves of two pioneer author-naturalists: **Richard Jefferies** (1848-87), who died at Goring-by-Sea, where he had lived for a short time; and **William Henry Hudson** (1841-1922), who wrote several books on birds and the countryside. The gateway to the cemetery has a plaque to both writers erected by the Sussex Wildlife Trust and the Royal Society for the Protection of Birds, and there is a memorial garden to the left of the entrance.

WARWICKSHIRE
BIRMINGHAM
The ashes of the Quaker chocolate manufacturer and social reformer **George Cadbury** (1839-1922) are kept in an urn at the Friends' meeting house, The Green, Bournville. He joined his father's Birmingham cocoa factory in 1856, moving the works to Bournville in 1879 and building a model village there to house the workers in 1893-1900.

Joseph Chamberlain (1836-1914), industrialist, politician and Mayor of Birmingham 1873-6, was buried in Key Hill Cemetery, also known as Birmingham General Cemetery, Icknield Street, B18; there is also an entrance on Key Hill. His grave is in the Unitarian section of the cemetery, marked by a large stone slab. Also at Key Hill, buried beside her mother, is the writer **Harriet Martineau** (1802-76).

At St Bartholomew, Church Road, Edgbaston, is the grave of **William Withering** (1741-99), the physician and botanist whose investigation of the foxglove was a turning point in the history of modern pharmacology. He was chief physician to Birmingham General Hospital and used the foxglove leaf, 'digitalis', in treatment. There is a wall monument, dating from 1808, in the outer south aisle; it shows a sprig of foxglove.

The graves of the engineers **Matthew Boulton** (1728-1809), his partner **James Watt** (1736-1819) and Boulton's protégé **William Murdock** (1754-1839), who all worked at Boulton & Watt's Soho Engineering Works in Handsworth, are at the church of St Mary, Church Hill, Handsworth. There are busts of Boulton and Murdock in the chancel, while there is a large statue of Watt in the very plain Watt Chapel.

In the churchyard of St Peter, Old Church Lane, Harborne, is the grave of the landscape painter **David Cox** (1783-1859). Cox, the son of a Birmingham blacksmith, was drawing master at Dulwich before returning to the Birmingham area in 1841.

Joseph Chamberlain was cartooned in 'a coat of many colours' to reflect the changes in his political thinking.

John Baskerville (1706-75), the Birmingham printer and typefounder, was originally buried in the mill which he had built beside his house, but this was destroyed during riots in 1791 and the coffin eventually came to rest in the vaults under the chapel at Warstone Lane Cemetery, Icknield Street, B18 (there is also an entrance on Warstone Lane). However, the chapel was demolished around 1955 and, although the vault remains, there is no monument visible.

CLAVERDON
Sir Francis Galton (1822-1911), founder of the 'science' of eugenics, is buried in a family vault at St Michael.

COVENTRY
The serial killer **Frederick West** (1941-95) of Gloucester hanged himself in jail on New Year's Day 1995 before he could be tried, although he had admitted to killing twelve young women and girls. He was cremated in March 1995 at Canley Crematorium, Cannon Hill Road, Coventry.

OLD MILVERTON
One-third of the ashes of the writer and feminist **Vera Mary Brittain** (1893-

1970) are buried in the churchyard of St James, Old Milverton, just north of Royal Leamington Spa. Brittain shares the grave with her husband, the political philosopher **Sir George Catlin** (1896-1979). Her remaining ashes are interred in Italy.

REDNAL
Cardinal John Henry Newman (1801-90), the leading Tractarian who became a Roman Catholic in 1845, is buried in the Oratory Graveyard at St Mary's Retreat, Rednal, with other fathers of the Oratory of St Philip Neri. Newman established the retreat house for use by congregation members from the Birmingham Oratory, which he founded in 1847. He shares his grave with an old friend, Ambrose St John.

STRATFORD-UPON-AVON
The playwright **William Shakespeare** (1564-1616), who was born and brought up in Stratford-upon-Avon, was buried by the north wall of the chancel of Holy Trinity; the grave of his wife **Anne Hathaway** (1556?-1623) is just to the left.
The popular novelist Mary Mackay (1855-1924), who wrote under the pseudonym **Marie Corelli**, settled in Stratford-upon-Avon in 1901. She died at her home, Mason Croft, in Church Street and was buried in the town's Evesham Road cemetery; her grave is marked by a large statue of an angel.

WARWICK
Robert Dudley (1532?-88), Earl of Leicester, favourite of Queen Elizabeth I, was buried in the Beauchamp Chapel of St Mary's church. Dudley's home was nearby at Kenilworth Castle, which had been given to him in 1563 by the Queen; he entertained the Queen with masques at the castle in 1575.
(John) **Enoch Powell** (1912-98), the politician and scholar notorious for his views on immigration, was buried in Warwick Cemetery. He had two funeral services, the first at St Margaret's church, Westminster, where he had been a churchwarden for ten years; the service included part of his own translation of St Matthew's Gospel. His body was then driven to St Mary's, the church of his old regiment, the Royal Warwickshire, for a second service, after which he was played from the church to the sound of Elgar's Imperial March. Powell was buried in his brigadier's uniform, with the poems he wrote for his wife Pamela.

WILTSHIRE
ALVEDISTON
The home of **(Robert) Anthony Eden** (1897-1977), first Earl of Avon, prime minister 1955-7, was at Alvediston, where he died. He was buried at St Mary; his grave is at the edge of the churchyard near the car park.

BRADFORD-ON-AVON
Henry Shrapnel (1761-1842), inventor of the Shrapnel shell, was born in Bradford-on-Avon; his home was Midway Manor House, which stands just to the south of the town. He was buried in the family vault in the chancel of Holy Trinity church.

BROAD CHALKE
In 1930 the photographer and designer **Sir Cecil Walter Hardy Beaton** (1904-80) rented Ashcombe, a derelict house in the Wiltshire Downs, which he converted into an idyllic home. He later moved to Reddish House, Broad Chalke, where he died. He was buried in the churchyard of All Saints; he has a blue slate headstone.

BROAD TOWN
The poet **Geoffrey Edward Harvey Grigson** (1905-85) is buried in the churchyard at Christ Church, beside his wife, the distinguished cookery writer **Jane Grigson**

(1928-90). The small village had been their home for many years. Their plain rounded headstones are 20 yards (18 metres) north-west of the church, close to the boundary.

BROMHAM
Thomas Moore (1779-1852), 'Ireland's greatest lyric poet', moved to Wiltshire in 1817 at the invitation of Lord Landsdowne of Bowood and lived for over thirty years in Sloperton Cottage, Bromham, with his wife Bessie. He is buried in the churchyard under a massive Celtic cross, some 20 feet (6 metres) high, by the north wall of the church. The east 'Bessie' window, to his widow, is by William Morris and Edward Burne-Jones.

HARDENHUISH
The economist **David Ricardo** (1772-1823) was buried in the churchyard of St Nicholas, beneath an elaborate Greek canopy (supported by four naked maidens) near the south-east corner of the church. Having made his fortune on the Stock Exchange, Ricardo eventually settled in Gloucestershire, buying the Gatcombe Park estate in late 1813.

LACOCK
The pioneer of photography **William Henry Fox Talbot** (1800-77), whose home was Lacock Abbey (which had been in the Talbot family since the sixteenth century), was buried at Lacock cemetery. His grave, which is shared by his wife, son and grand-daughter, is by the path on the right of the cemetery and is marked by a large headstone.

NEWTON TONEY
Celia Fiennes (1662-1741) was born in the manor house at Newton Toney, near Salisbury. Her accounts of her travels throughout England on horseback during 1685-1710 provide a splendid picture of the state of the nation. In her later years she lived in London, but in her will she specified arrangements for her eventual burial at Newton Toney.

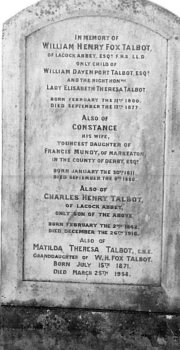

OARE
The art historian and communist spy **Anthony Frederick Blunt** (1907-83) was a pupil at Marlborough College, 4 miles (6 km) north of Oare, in the 1920s. In 1926 he published a poem in *The Marlburian* about the ridge of Wiltshire downland which ran to the south of the school, where Blunt and his brothers had all enjoyed walking. Anthony Blunt died in London and was cremated at Putney Vale Cemetery. Shortly afterwards, his brothers Wilfrid and Christopher Blunt scattered his ashes on

The headstone of the photographic pioneer William Henry Fox Talbot and his family at Lacock cemetery. In 1846 Fox Talbot published 'The Pencil of Nature', the first book illustrated without the help of an artist; his plain headstone, however, does not reflect the creativity of his career.

the slopes of that same ridge, topped by an ancient hillfort and known as Martinsell Hill, which is a mile (just over a kilometre) north-east of Oare.

SEVENHAMPTON

The thriller writer **Ian Lancaster Fleming** (1908-64), creator of secret agent '007' James Bond, bought Warneford Place, Sevenhampton, in 1959. It was the country house his wife had always desired, and they moved in four years later, after much building work. Fleming was buried at the parish church, St Andrew, in an unmarked grave; his wife and son were also buried in the churchyard.

TOLLARD ROYAL

The anthropologist and archaeologist **Augustus Henry Lane Fox Pitt-Rivers** (1827-1900), whose original surname was Fox, assumed the name Pitt-Rivers on inheriting the estates of his great-uncle, George Pitt, second Baron Rivers, in 1880. The estates were based around the large house known as Rushmore, just east of Tollard Royal, where Pitt-Rivers lived from 1880. His collection of articles relating to human evolution, which he kept at his London home, was presented to Oxford University in 1883 and placed in the Pitt-Rivers Museum. Pitt-Rivers was buried in St Peter ad Vincula at Tollard Royal, where there is a commemorative marble tablet.

TROWBRIDGE

The poet **George Crabbe** (1754-1832) was vicar of Trowbridge from 1814 until his death in 1832. He was buried in the chancel of St James, where his monument shows him lying on his deathbed, Bible in hand, while angels hover above.

WORCESTERSHIRE

DUDLEY

The England and Manchester United footballer **Duncan Edwards** (1938-58), who died in the Munich air crash, is buried next to his sister at Queen's Cross Cemetery.

EVESHAM

Simon de Montfort (1208?-65), Earl of Leicester and the creator of a forerunner of the House of Commons, was killed in the battle of Evesham. He was buried by the

The stone at Evesham marking the burial site of Simon de Montfort came from his castle in France and was unveiled by the Speaker of the House of Commons on the seven hundreth anniversary of de Montfort's death.

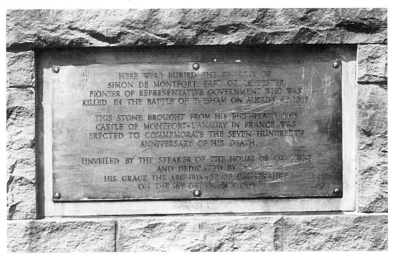

high altar at Evesham Abbey, which is now in ruins; there is a stone in the Abbey Gardens on its site.

GREAT MALVERN

The singer **Johanna Maria ('Jenny') Lind** (1820-87), 'the Swedish Nightingale', is buried at the cemetery, Great Malvern. Her grave, under a carved pedestal surmounted by a cross, is surrounded by low railings, 35 yards (30 metres) north of the chapel door. Lind lived at Wynds Point near Little Malvern, towards the southern end of the Malvern Hills, about 4 miles (6 km) from Great Malvern.

GRIMLEY

The ashes of **Sir Samuel White Baker** (1821-93), the traveller and sportsman who was one of the great explorers of East Africa, were buried in the churchyard of St Bartholomew. The Baker family tomb is under the trees east of the church path.

HALESOWEN

The poet and landscape gardener **William Shenstone** (1714-63) was born at the Leasowes, an estate just over a mile (2 km) north-east of Halesowen. He inherited

Sir Edward Elgar intended that his ashes should be scattered in the rivers Severn and Teme, but his wishes were overruled by his family – Roman Catholics (as was Elgar) – who were against cremation. He was eventually buried beside his wife (who had died nearly fourteen years earlier) in St Wulfstan's churchyard at Little Malvern.

the estate in 1745 and spent most of his life there, improving the grounds at great expense in the Picturesque manner. He was buried in the churchyard of the parish church, St John Baptist; a plain tombstone marks his grave.

LITTLE MALVERN

The composer **Sir Edward William Elgar** (1857-1934) was the son of a Worcester organist and music seller. Elgar, a Roman Catholic, always loved the Malvern Hills but moved from Hereford to London in 1912, returning to live in Worcestershire in 1923. He had intended that his ashes should be scattered at the confluence of the rivers Severn and Teme, just south of Worcester, but his family decided that he should be buried beside his wife in St Wulstan's Roman Catholic churchyard, Wells Road, Little Malvern.

WEST MALVERN

Peter Mark Roget (1779-1869), the physician who published *Roget's Thesaurus of English Words and Phrases* in 1852, died at West Malvern on his annual holiday at Ashfield House, West Malvern Road. He was buried in the churchyard of St James under a polished grey ledger, fifteen paces from the war memorial.

WORCESTER

John (1167?-1216), king of England, who was called Lackland in his youth, was buried in the chancel of Worcester Cathedral. His monument is a fine Purbeck marble effigy, in which he is accompanied by a pair of sturdy bishops. **Stanley Baldwin** (1867-1947), first Earl Baldwin of Bewdley, prime minister 1923-4, 1924-9 and 1935-7, was born in Bewdley, 10 miles (16 km) north-west of Worcester. He was the son of a Worcestershire ironmaster and lived at Wilden, just south of Bewdley, for several years before his marriage. Baldwin was MP for West Worcestershire during 1908-37, and his Worcestershire home was at Astley Hall, Astley (midway between Bewdley and Worcester). He died at Astley Hall and his ashes were laid with those of his wife, who had died in 1945, in the nave of Worcester Cathedral, by the west entrance. The novelist **Francis Brett Young** (1884-1954) lived at Fladbury, near Evesham, from 1932 until 1945, when he left for South Africa. He wrote several books whilst at Fladbury, setting many of them in the Worcester area. His ashes were interred in Worcester Cathedral.

YORKSHIRE, EAST

KINGSTON UPON HULL

The funeral service for the poet **Philip Arthur Larkin** (1922-85), who was Librarian of Hull University during 1955-85, was held at St Mary the Virgin, Hallgate, Cottingham, the University church. Larkin was buried in Cottingham Cemetery, a short distance from the church in Eppleworth Road. There is a plain white gravestone inscribed with his name, dates and the word 'Writer'.

LONDESBOROUGH

The gentleman architect **Richard Boyle, third Earl of Burlington** and fourth Earl of Cork (1695-1753), was buried in the family vault at All Saints. His sole visible monument is an inscribed brass plate, which was originally fixed to the coffin. The site of the family seat, Londesborough Hall (pulled down in 1818-19), was just south-east of the church.

RUDSTON

Near the western edge of the churchyard of All Saints, almost directly across from the south wall of the church, is the grave of the writer **Winifred Holtby**

The grave of the writer and feminist Winifred Holtby (1898-1935) in Rudston churchyard is marked by a memorial in the form of an open book, which bears the epitaph 'God give me work till my life shall end, and life till my work is done'.

(1898-1935), whose *South Riding* was published in 1936. Aptly, it is marked by an almost white headstone in the form of an open book. Holtby was born and brought up in Rudston.

SCRAYINGHAM

The 'Railway King', **George Hudson** (1800-71), was buried in the churchyard of St Peter. His gravestone lies south-west of the porch with others from the Hudson family. Hudson was the son of a Yorkshire farmer, made his fortune as a draper at York and then began his career as a railway tycoon.

YORKSHIRE, NORTH

BILBROUGH

The home of the commander-in-chief of the Parliamentary Army, General **Thomas Fairfax** (1612-71), third Baron Fairfax of Cameron, was Nunappleton House, 4 miles (6 km) south-east of Bilbrough. He was buried in a side chapel of Bilbrough parish church.

BOLTON-ON-SWALE

The massive and curiously shaped obelisk in the churchyard of St Mary, just west of the church, marks the grave of **Henry Jenkins** (d.1670), 'the Modern Methuselah'. Jenkins lived a little way south of the village, at Ellerton-upon-Swale, and claimed to have been born around 1501. His 169 years are commemorated both by the obelisk, erected in 1743, and by a memorial inside the beautifully decorated church.

COXWOLD

The writer **Laurence Sterne** (1713-68), who published the initial parts of *Tristram Shandy* in 1759, was the great-grandson of an Archbishop of York. He became curate of Coxwold in 1760 and his home in the village, until his death, was Shandy

The obelisk (dating from 1743) in the churchyard of St Mary, Bolton-on-Swale, commemorates 'the modern Methuselah', Henry Jenkins (d.1670), who is said to have lived 169 years.

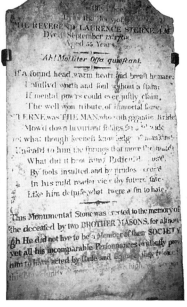

Hall. Sterne was buried in London, in a graveyard behind Hyde Park Place, Bayswater Road, which is now a school playground. His body was stolen by body-snatchers but recognised and returned; however, it was removed to Coxwold in 1969 by the Sterne Trust. It was re-buried in the churchyard of St Michael, outside the south wall of the nave, just east of the porch; the exact spot is not marked. Sterne's original headstone is displayed inside the porch. Also buried at St Michael, under the floor of the chancel, was **Lord Adolphus FitzClarence** (1802-56), younger son of King William IV by his mistress, Mrs Jordan. He died while visiting nearby Newburgh Priory; there is a memorial tablet on the south side of the chancel.

Laurence Sterne's original headstone was brought from London to Coxwold by the Sterne Trust and is now mounted inside the south porch of St Michael's church.

FELIXKIRK

The veterinary surgeon Alf Wight (1916-95), who as **James Herriot** wrote the books about a Yorkshire vet that were made into the television series *All Creatures Great and Small*, was buried at Felixkirk, near his home. Wight worked as a vet in Thirsk, 2 miles (3 km) south-west of the village.

HUBBERHOLME

The playwright and novelist **John Boynton Priestley** (1894-1984) was born and brought up in Bradford. He visited Hubberholme in the course of his *English Journey* (1934) and had lunch at the inn opposite the church of St Michael and All Angels. He was impressed with the 'cosy inn', which provided soup, Yorkshire pudding, roast chicken and sausages, fruit pudding, cheese and biscuits, and coffee, all for two shillings and sixpence. J. B. Priestley's ashes were buried in Hubberholme churchyard, and there is a memorial plaque inside the church.

SCARBOROUGH

The novelist **Anne Brontë** (1820-49) came to Scarborough for the good of her health but died in the resort. She was buried at St Mary, Castle Road, in the eastern extension of the churchyard (beyond the ruined part of the church); her grave is towards its north side.

SPOFFORTH

John Metcalf (1717-1810), known as 'Blind Jack of Knaresborough', became blind at the age of six but was a distinguished athlete and pioneer road-builder. He retired to a small farm in 1792 and was buried in the churchyard of All Saints at Spofforth, about 3 miles (5 km) south of Knaresborough.

TERRINGTON

The grave of the historian **Arnold Joseph Toynbee** (1889-1975) is at the burial ground in Terrington, near his Yorkshire home on the edge of the Howardian Hills.

YORK

William Fitzherbert (d.1154), Archbishop of York, generally known as **St William of York**, was originally buried at the east end of the nave of York Minster. His remains were

Anne Brontë's grave in the churchyard extension at St Mary, Scarborough. Anne was the youngest of the three Brontë sisters; Emily and Charlotte were buried at Haworth, where their father was curate, and there is a memorial tablet to all three sisters in Poets' Corner, Westminster Abbey, not far from Shakespeare's monument. It was presented by the Brontë Society and unveiled in 1947.

moved to a shrine behind the high altar after his canonisation in 1227, but the shrine was demolished in 1541. His coffin was rediscovered in 1732 and again in 1968 and was then removed to the western crypt.

The highwayman **Richard 'Dick' Turpin** (1706-39) was hanged at York and

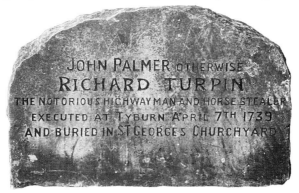

The unprepossessing headstone of the highwayman Dick Turpin, who was born in Essex, the son of an innkeeper. After preying on travellers around London for many years, he moved to the north of England, where he became known as John Palmer, after his mother's surname. He was eventually arrested for horse stealing and hanged at York.

buried in the churchyard of the old St George's church (which has long gone) on George Street. The churchyard is now an uninspiring public garden, where Turpin's small headstone still survives, the only upright stone amongst many flat slabs.

The artist **William Etty** (1787-1849), famous for his paintings of nudes, was born and brought up in York although he spent most of his career in London. He

returned to York in 1848, buying a house on Coney Street, and died there the following year. He was buried in the churchyard of St Olave, Marygate, as he had requested; his large tomb-chest stands at the far south-eastern edge of the churchyard, by the ruined walls of St Mary's Abbey.

The Quaker cocoa manufacturer and philanthropist **Joseph Rowntree** (1836-1925) is buried at the Society of Friends burial ground, Heslington Road, along with his father **Joseph Rowntree** (1801-59), who opened the original grocery shop in York in 1822. The firm that grew from this small

The chest tomb of the artist William Etty (1787-1849) stands in St Olave's churchyard, York, beside the ruined walls of St Mary's Abbey. Etty, the son of a local miller and confectioner, campaigned for the conservation of York's ancient buildings.

The Rowntree family graves in the corner of the Society of Friends burial ground at York. This peaceful burial ground was created in 1855 from part of the estate of The Retreat, a Quaker mental institution, on Heslington Road.

beginning became a limited company in 1897, when the works moved to Haxby Road, on the northern edge of York. The burial ground lies at the south-east corner of the splendidly spacious gardens of Lamel Beeches (limited public access). The graves of the Rowntree family are grouped together in the north-west corner of this secluded and peaceful burial ground, which contains row upon row of small headstones identical but for their inscriptions.

York Cemetery, Cemetery Road, was laid out in 1836-7. The grave of **George Townsend Andrews** (1805-55), the architect who designed many railway stations for his friend and political associate George Hudson, the 'Railway King', is near the centre of the cemetery. To find it, take the main, broad path leading from the gatehouse on Cemetery Road, immediately passing (on the left) the headstone of **Frank Buck** (1904-66), local scrap dealer and vintage car enthusiast. Carved on the top of his white headstone is an exact image of a saloon car, complete with registration number FB 600. Continue along the broad path to the chapel. Here turn left and quickly right along a curving grass path. Soon, a large squirrel – carved into the top of a tree trunk – is seen on the left, amongst the flowers; the grave of G. T. Andrews is just north of this point. The flat stone slab, with its delicate raised cross, is now almost completely obscured by ivy.

YORKSHIRE, SOUTH
EDLINGTON

Arthur Wharton (1865-1930) was a world record sprinter and Britain's first black professional footballer; he was also the first black Amateur Athletic Associa-

A most unusual modern monument, complete with horn and number plate, to the vintage car enthusiast Frank Buck at York Cemetery. The headstone also commemorates his wife Margaret and their son Albert, who put up the memorial, one of the first to be seen on entering the cemetery.

tion champion. He was born in Accra (now in Ghana) but came to study in England when young, eventually appearing in an FA Cup semi-final for Preston North End (1887) and playing in the then First Division with Sheffield United. After his sporting career was over, he worked as a haulage hand at the Yorkshire Main Colliery at Edlington, on the south-western outskirts of Doncaster. He died in Doncaster and was buried in an unmarked grave in Edlington Cemetery, Edlington Lane, New Edlington. A polished black headstone with gold lettering was erected over the grave in 1997, after research into Wharton's life had revealed its existence.

YORKSHIRE, WEST

HAWORTH

The authors **Charlotte Brontë** (1816-55) and **Emily Jane Brontë** (1818-48), with their brother **Patrick Branwell Brontë** (1817-48), lie in the family vault of the old church of St Michael, where their father was curate. Their home was the nearby parsonage. A plaque at the south-east end of the nave of the church (rebuilt in 1880-1) marks the site of the vault.

HEPTONSTALL

The poet **Sylvia Plath** (1932-63) is buried in the churchyard of the new church of St Thomas at Heptonstall; the small hilltop village is in Calderdale, the area where her husband, the poet Ted Hughes, spent his youth.

LEEDS

The civil engineer **John Smeaton** (1724-92), builder of the third Eddystone lighthouse in 1756-9, was born at Austhorpe, on the eastern edge of Leeds. After his marriage in 1756 he spent most of his life at his home in Austhorpe, where he built a detached four-storey tower fitted up as a workshop and study. He died at Austhorpe and was buried in the chancel of the parish church, St Mary's in Whitkirk, just west of Austhorpe. Smeaton's memorial tablet is topped by a depiction of the Eddystone lighthouse.

SALTAIRE

The textile manufacturer and philanthropist **Sir Titus Salt** (1803-76) began to move his factory from central Bradford to the countryside at Saltaire, 3 miles (5 km) to the north-west, in 1851. He built up a model township around the new mill, adding the splendid Congregational church, George Street, in 1859. Salt, an ardent Congregationalist, was buried in the family mausoleum, which stands beside his church.

The industrialist and philanthropist Sir Titus Salt (1803-76) was buried in the family mausoleum which stands beside the Congregational church in his model village of Saltaire, West Yorkshire. Salt, who made his fortune from alpaca wool, was an ardent Congregationalist and gave the church to Saltaire; he also donated several sites in the village for the construction of churches of other faiths. There were, however, no public houses.

123

Channel Islands

ALDERNEY

The broadcaster, journalist and connoisseur **John Arlott** (1914-91) is buried in St Anne's churchyard on the island of Alderney. Arlott was a member of the BBC radio ball-by-ball cricket commentary team from 1946 until his retirement in 1980, after which he moved to Alderney, seeking clean air (for his health), sea and solitude.

JERSEY

The grave of the showman and holiday camp magnate **Sir William Heygate Edmund Colborne ('Billy') Butlin** (1899-1980) can be found in St John's Cemetery, St Helier. Butlin retired and moved to Jersey for tax reasons in 1968, having handed over the running of his company to his son, Robert. He died at Blair Adam House, his Jersey home; the funeral was the biggest ever seen in Jersey. Butlin was buried, in a site he chose himself, dressed in a blue suit with brown shoes, in accordance with the fairground showman's tradition. Holiday images decorate his massive polished black granite tomb, which the Butlin family liken in shape to a double bed.

In the churchyard of St Saviour is the grave of the 'Jersey Lily', the actress **Emilie Charlotte 'Lillie' Langtry** (1853-1929), daughter of the Dean of Jersey. Langtry, who was born at St Saviour's rectory, was mistress of the Prince of Wales during the late 1870s, before taking up her acting career. She bought a villa in the south of France after the First World War and died at Monte Carlo. Her grave, well signposted, is surmounted by her marble bust.

Scotland

BORDERS

CHIRNSIDE

The motor-racing driver **James 'Jim' Clark** (1936-68), world champion in 1963 and 1965, was born in Fife but moved to the Borders with his family when he was six. He worked as a shepherd on his father's farm before taking up racing full-time. He was made the first honorary burgess of Duns, 5 miles (8 km) west of Chirnside, in 1965. His grave is in the kirkyard at Chirnside.

COLDSTREAM

Alexander Frederick 'Alec' Douglas-Home (1903-95), Lord Home of the Hirsel, prime minister 1963-4, was born at Coldstream on his family's estate. He died at Coldstream and was buried in the family plot in the local churchyard.

DRYBURGH

The novelist **Sir Walter Scott** (1771-1832) is buried in a granite sarcophagus in the north transept of Dryburgh Abbey, known as St Mary's Aisle. The abbey and its lands had belonged to Scott's great-grandfather, but by Scott's day all that remained of the inheritance was the right of burial in the abbey. Scott's home from 1812 until his death was Abbotsford, 4 miles (6 km) north-west of Dryburgh. Also buried at Dryburgh Abbey, at his own request, was **Douglas Haig** (1861-1928), first Earl Haig, field marshal, who came from a famous Borders family. In 1921 he was presented by public subscription with the ancestral home of the Haigs, Bemersyde, which stood only a mile (nearly 2 km) north of the abbey.

ETTRICK

The poet **James Hogg** (1770-1835), known as 'the Ettrick Shepherd', was born in Ettrick. He was granted Moss End Farm, close to the Yarrow Water and about 5 miles (8 km) north of Ettrick in 1815, and it became his main home for the rest of his life. He was buried in the kirkyard at Ettrick; his headstone has a carving of a harp.

MELROSE

The heart of **Robert Bruce** (1274-1329), King Robert I and liberator of Scotland, was buried at Melrose Ab-

Dryburgh Abbey, the burial place of Sir Walter Scott and Field Marshal Earl Haig, occupies a secluded and beautiful site on a horseshoe bend of the Tweed. Scott's granite sarcophagus, which stands in St Mary's Aisle, had become a tourist attraction by the end of the nineteenth century. Haig's simple military tombstone was carved by Pilkington Jackson. The abbey is in the care of Historic Scotland.

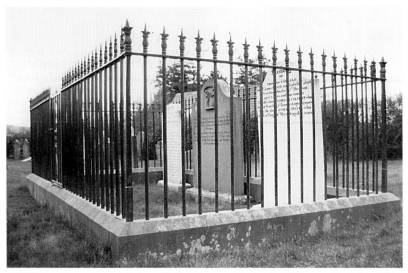

Within railings at his birthplace, Ecclefechan, are the tombs of Thomas Carlyle and his family. He had expressed a wish to be buried here rather than in Westminster Abbey, as had been suggested.

bey, after it had been taken on a Crusade to the Holy Land, as was Bruce's wish; his body was buried at Dunfermline Abbey.

CENTRAL

BALQUHIDDER

The Highland freebooter Robert Macgregor (1671-1734), commonly known as **Rob Roy**, died at home and was buried in the kirkyard beneath an old cross-slab, beside his wife and two sons.

CAMBUSKENNETH

James III (1451-88), king of Scotland, was murdered after losing the battle at Sauchieburn and buried in the kirkyard at Cambuskenneth. His monument was erected in 1865 at the command of Queen Victoria, after his remains had been discovered.

DUMFRIES AND GALLOWAY

DUMFRIES

The poet **Robert Burns** (1759-96) settled in Dumfries in 1791 after giving up farming. He was buried in the north-east corner of the kirkyard at St Michael's church, St Michael Street. The grave was moved to the south-east corner in 1815, in order that a large domed mausoleum could be erected in his memory. The white-painted octagonal structure houses Burns, his wife and five of their sons, as well as his original memorial stone, a flat red sandstone slab which was placed on his grave about 1805.

ECCLEFECHAN

The writer and historian **Thomas Carlyle** (1795-1881) was the son of an Ecclefechan mason and went to the parish school. He is buried in the kirkyard beside his parents, within a railed enclosure. A sign points the way.

LANGHOLM

The poet Christopher Murray Grieve (1892-1978), who wrote under the pseudonym **Hugh MacDiarmid**, was born and educated at Langholm; he was buried at Langholm cemetery.

MOFFAT

John Loudon McAdam (1756-1836), the 'macadamiser' of roads, is buried at the Old Churchyard, Selkirk Road, in a railed grave just north of the remains of the old church. McAdam lived on the Dumcrieff estate about a mile (nearly 2 km) south-east of Moffat, although he conducted many of his road-making experiments in the south-west of England.

PARTON

James Clerk-Maxwell (1831-79), the experimental physicist best known for his research into electromagnetism, is buried in the kirkyard by the ruins of the old parish church, on the edge of the hamlet where he grew up.

FIFE

DUNFERMLINE

Robert Bruce (1274-1329), King Robert I and liberator of Scotland, died of leprosy and his body was buried at Dunfermline Abbey. His heart, which he had asked to be taken to Jerusalem, was indeed taken to the Holy Land but was eventually buried at Melrose Abbey. The exact site of Bruce's grave at Dunfermline has been lost, although it is supposedly behind the altar of the parish church (a continuation of the abbey church). A brass incised with his full-size figure was set under the pulpit of the parish church in 1889. **Robert Stewart** (1340?-1420), first Duke of Albany, regent of Scotland, was also buried at Dunfermline.

EAST WEMYSS

A splendid monument in the south-west corner of Macduff Cemetery, Shand Terrace, designed by Charles Rennie Mackintosh, is a severely flattened cross in Dullatur sandstone. The cross encloses an oval, in which a dove flies above the copper inscription panel (a replacement dating from around 1950). It commemorates a local minister, the **Reverend Alexander Orrock Johnston** (1840-1905).

KIRKCALDY

The child author and prodigy **Marjorie Fleming** (1803-11), 'the Youngest Immortal in the World of Letters', was buried in the kirkyard of Abbotshall church, Abbotshall Road, in the centre of Kirkcaldy, the town where she was born. Whilst staying with an aunt, she wrote a journal that was eventually published as *Pet Marjorie* (1858). Her grave, to the south of the church, is marked by a memorial featuring her seated with the journal open upon her knee; the statue was erected in 1930.

ST ANDREWS

The scholar **Andrew Lang** (1844-1912) was educated at St Andrews University. He eventually settled in London but returned to live at St Andrews; his grave in the east cemetery is marked by a Celtic cross.

GRAMPIAN

SPYNIE

The Labour Party leader **James Ramsay Macdonald** (1866-1937), prime minister 1924, 1929-31 and 1931-5, was born at Lossiemouth, 3 miles (5 km) north of the tiny hamlet of Spynie. He was buried in the kirkyard at Spynie, beside the ashes of his wife, the socialist activist **Margaret Macdonald** (1870-1911).

HIGHLAND

KILMUIR (SKYE)

The Jacobite heroine **Flora Macdonald** (1722-90), who assisted Prince Charles Edward Stuart (Bonnie Prince Charlie) to escape to Skye following his defeat at Culloden, emigrated to North Carolina in 1774 but returned home to Skye in 1779.

She is buried in the north-west corner of the kirkyard at Kilmuir, near the northern-most tip of the island. Her grave is marked by a tall plain Celtic cross in grey granite, dating from 1880.

SANDAIG

The naturalist and author **Gavin Maxwell** (1914-69) lived from time to time after 1949 in a cottage at Sandaig, on a small bay at the western end of the remote Knoydart peninsula. There he wrote *Ring of Bright Water* (1960), which described the otters who shared his home. The cottage burnt down in 1968 and Maxwell died the following year; his ashes were buried under a stone slab marking the site of the cottage.

LOTHIAN

EDINBURGH

The kings of Scotland **David II** (1324-71) or David Bruce, **James II** (1430-60) and **James V** (1512-42) were buried at Holyrood Abbey in the royal vault. This occupies the south-east corner inside the abbey's east end. David II was the first king to be buried at Holyrood.

Lord James Stewart (1531?-70), Earl of Mar, and afterwards Earl of Moray, half-brother of Mary, Queen of Scots, was buried at St Giles Cathedral on High Street. The plain grey monument to the Earl of Moray, 'the Good Regent', is in a small aisle leading off the south side of the church, just west of the organ. Buried in the vaults in 1661 (eleven years after his execution) are the remains of Charles I's champion in Scotland, **James Graham, Marquis of Montrose** (1612-50), who defeated the Covenant army in several battles. His effigy and monument were erected in 1888. **John Knox** (1505-72), minister and reformer, was buried in St Giles churchyard some time after it was officially closed. Knox was minister at St Giles, and the site of his grave is in Parliament Square, just south of St Giles. It is probably under parking space 44, which is towards the eastern end.

The philosopher and historian **David Hume** (1711-76) was born and educated in Edinburgh and was buried at Old Calton Cemetery, which is entered from Waterloo Place. His splendid monument is at the south-west corner of the inner section of the burial ground.

Robert Stevenson (1772-1850) and his sons **Thomas Stevenson** (1818-87) and **Alan Stevenson** (1807-65), the family of lighthouse designers and builders, are all buried at the New Calton Cemetery, on Regent Road. Their walled grave is halfway along the eastern edge of the cemetery, just outside the path. Robert Stevenson was the grandfather of the writer Robert Louis Stevenson.

The political economist **Adam Smith** (1723-90), who published *The Wealth of Nations* in 1776, retired to Panmure House in Canongate. He was buried in Canongate Kirkyard; his grave is to the left as you enter the kirkyard, immediately behind the wall of the Canongate Tolbooth, and is enclosed by high black railings. By the outside wall of Canongate kirk is the grave of **David Rizzio** (1533?-66), private secretary to Mary, Queen of Scots; he was murdered at Holyrood Palace.

Take the path along the northern edge of Greyfriars kirkyard, entered from Candlemaker Row, and bear left slightly at its end to find the mausoleum of the Adam family, the architects, who lived nearby in Chambers Street. There is a bust of **William Adam** (1689-1748), the leading Scottish architect and father of Robert Adam, who is buried in Westminster Abbey. The grave of **James Hutton** (1726-97), 'the Father of Modern Geology', who lived in Edinburgh for most of his life, is in the northern extension to the kirkyard, through the gate to the left of the Adam mausoleum. To find the grave, walk about halfway along the extension, then go through a gate on the left; the site is marked by a white marble plaque. Also buried at Greyfriars, but in an unmarked grave, is 'the world's worst poet', **William McGonagall** (1825-1902), who lived nearby on Cowgate.

John Napier (1550-1617), the inventor of logarithms as well as an early attempt at a calculating machine, is buried in St Cuthbert's church, off Princes Street. His finely carved wall monument is at the west end of the church, near its south-west corner. The writer **Thomas De Quincey** (1785-1859), who published *Confessions of an English Opium Eater* in 1822 and settled in Edinburgh in 1828, is buried in St Cuthbert's churchyard. To find his grave, ascend the steps just south-west of the west end of the church, climbing past walled tombs and up a short incline to a wall. The eighth grave along to the left, which has a headstone with a semicircular top, is De Quincey's.

Elsie Maud Inglis (1864-1917), the physician, surgeon and suffragist who founded the Scottish Women's Hospitals Committee in 1914, is buried at the Dean Cemetery, Dean Path, Dean. Also here is the architect **William Henry Playfair** (1789-1857), who designed many of Edinburgh's best-known buildings. His grave is in the southern section of the cemetery, at its western extremity, and is marked by a plain white altar. It can be found by taking the path directly west from the main gate and following it to the T-junction. The grave is a few plots to the left on the far side of the perimeter path.

WHITTINGEHAME
Arthur James Balfour (1848-1930), first Earl of Balfour, prime minister 1902-5, was born at Whittingehame and is buried in the Balfour family plot in the kirkyard.

ORKNEY

HARRAY
The novelist **Eric Robert Russell Linklater** (1899-1974), whose father was an Orcadian, spent his summer holidays on the Orkney Islands from a very young age. Linklater lived on the Orkneys, at Harray on West Mainland, during 1933-47, and was buried in Harray parish kirkyard. His grave is marked by a very tall standing stone.

ORKNEY ISLANDS
Horatio Herbert Kitchener (1850-1916), first Earl Kitchener of Khartoum and of Broome, field marshal, sailed for Russia from Scapa Flow in 1916 aboard the HMS *Hampshire*. The cruiser appears to have struck a mine in bad weather off the Orkneys and went down with most of the crew.

STRATHCLYDE

AUCHINLECK
James Boswell (1740-95), the biographer of Samuel Johnson, was the son of Lord Auchinleck. Initially the family home was Second Keep, 3 miles (5 km) west of the village, but they moved to his father's newly built Place Affleck at Auchinleck in 1762. Boswell, who eventually succeeded to the Auchinleck estates, visited the village for short spells in 1769 and 1773 but died in London. He and his wife are buried in the family mausoleum next to the village church.

GLASGOW
The grave of the Glasgow industrialist and philanthropist **David Dale** (1739-1806), who initiated the idea of the model industrial community at New Lanark, is at the New Burying Ground to the rear of St David's (Ramshorn) church, on Ingram Street in the centre of the city. Taking the path to the right of the church, which leads directly into the New Burying Ground, carry on beside the east wall, passing an intersection, until about halfway along; a wall tablet marks the grave.

At the Southern Necropolis, Caledonia Road, is the grave of **Sir Thomas Johnstone Lipton** (1850-1931), grocer and yachtsman, who was born in a Glasgow

The Boswell family mausoleum adjoins the church at Auchinleck. James Boswell and his wife are buried there.

tenement. In 1871 he opened in Glasgow the first of his series of grocery shops, which made him a millionaire by 1880. His tomb is in the east section of the necropolis, inside the path which runs along its Caledonia Street side, and just over halfway along from the central path towards the Caledonia Road. Lipton's tall polished granite headstone faces west and towers over a flat granite slab. Over in the western section of the necropolis is the grave of the Glasgow architect **Alexander Thomson** (1817-75), known as 'Greek Thomson' because of his penchant for that style. It is immediately to the east of the intersection of paths in the centre of the western section, but only the lower part of Thomson's memorial stone remains.

In the Western Necropolis, Tresta Road, Maryhill, is the grave of the socialist and Labour leader **(James) Keir Hardie** (1856-1915), who was born near Glasgow.

The football manager **John 'Jock' Stein** (1922-85), who successfully took charge of both Celtic and the Scottish national team, was cremated at the Linn Park Crematorium, Castle Road, Cathcart, on the southern edge of the city.

GREENOCK

The novelist **John Galt** (1779-1839) spent his youth at Greenock, where he was employed at the Customs House, before moving to London in 1804. He retired to Greenock in 1834 and died there in 1839. He is buried in the Old Cemetery, Inverkip Street, which is not normally open to the public.

IONA

The Labour Party leader **John Smith** (1938-94), who died suddenly less than two years after taking over the post, had spent many happy family holidays in a rented crofter's cottage on Iona and loved the island. He was buried in the churchyard of St Oran's Abbey, a remote and solitary spot (which has suffered recently from an excess of visitors). His gravestone lies on the east side of the narrow northern extension of the churchyard, near the abbey. The large dark flat slab bears the following epitaph in gold lettering: 'An honest man's the noblest work of God'.

ROTHESAY

John Stuart, third Earl of Bute (1713-92), prime minister 1762-3, dabbled in

The politician John Smith (1938-94), leader of the Labour Party at the time of his sudden death, is buried on the remote island of Iona, in the churchyard of St Oran's Abbey. His unusual gravestone (farthest away of the three), a rounded and highly polished rectangular slab, lies beside the churchyard's eastern wall; there are fine views of the abbey and the Sound of Iona, which separates the island from Mull.

agriculture, botany and architecture in his early years at the family estates centred around Mount Stuart House, to the south of Rothesay. In retirement he lived in Dorset, but after his death in 1792 his body was brought back to Bute for burial at Rothesay.

TAYSIDE

ARBROATH

William the Lyon (1143-1214), king of Scotland, founded the monastery of Arbroath in 1178 and was buried before the high altar of Arbroath Abbey.

KIRRIEMUIR

The playwright and novelist **Sir James Matthew Barrie** (1860-1937), author of *Peter Pan* (1904), was born in Kirriemuir. He was the son of a handloom weaver. Barrie went to London in 1884 but often returned to the town to visit his parents. He is buried with them at the New Church Cemetery, on its west side near the manse.

PERTH

James I (1394-1437), king of Scotland, was murdered at Perth and buried there in the convent of the Carthusians.

Margaret Tudor (1489-1541), queen of Scotland, died at Methven Castle, about 4 miles (6 km) north-west of Perth, and was buried in the church of St John at Perth.

J. M. Barrie

WESTERN ISLES

EOLIGARRY (BARRA)

The writer **Sir (Edward Montague) Compton Mackenzie** (1883-1972) lived on Barra during the Second World War. He set his successful novel *Whisky Galore* (1947) on the small island of Eriskay, just north-east of Barra. He is buried in the kirkyard at Eoligarry; his grave is close to the ruined church, which may have been dedicated to St Barr.

Wales

(arranged for convenience by pre-1997 counties)

CLWYD

COLWYN BAY

The philosopher and social reformer **Bertrand Arthur William Russell** (1872-1970), third Earl Russell, lived from 1954 until his death at Plas Penrhyn, near the small town of Penrhyndeudraeth, about 25 miles (40 km) south-west of Colwyn Bay, and close to the model Italian village of Portmeirion. He was cremated, with no ceremony (as was his wish), at the town crematorium in Colwyn Bay, and his ashes were simply scattered.

LLANGOLLEN

Plas Newydd, with its elaborate Gothic interiors, was the home for fifty years of the 'Ladies of Llangollen', **Lady Eleanor Butler** (1739?-1829) and the **Honourable Sarah Ponsonby** (1755-1831). They eloped together from Ireland in 1779, setting up home at Llangollen in their house on the hillside above the town, where

The Celtic cross of Charles Stewart Rolls at Llangattock-Vibon-Avel.

they were visited by many famous personages. They were keen on literary self-improvement and general eccentricity and transformed the house and grounds in a suitably romantic manner. They were both buried in the churchyard of St Collen, where there is a triangular Gothic tombstone, erected in 1809 following the death of their friend and housekeeper, Mary Caryll, who shares the grave. Inside the church is a monument dating from 1937, erected at the expense of the Ladies' biographer, the feminist Mary Gordon. It consists of a pair of relief portraits, for which Gordon and the sculptor, Violet Labouchere, were the models.

MOLD

In the churchyard of the parish church, close to the church wall, is the grave of the painter **Richard Wilson** (1714-82).

DYFED

KIDWELLY

Princess Gwenllian (1098-1136), daughter of the king of Gwynedd, may have been Britain's earliest known woman writer. She is said to be the author of the main tales from *The Mabinogion*, which tells of daring deeds in the Celtic world. She died leading an attack on the Normans at the battlefield Maes Gwenllian, near Kidwelly; the site has never been fully excavated and the exact location of her grave is unknown.

LAUGHARNE

The poet **Dylan Marlais Thomas** (1914-53) settled in Laugharne in 1949. He lived at The Boathouse, a whitewashed house below the cliff, and wrote in its garden shed; *Under Milk Wood* was published in 1954. He died in New York but was buried in the hillside churchyard of St Martin at Laugharne, where his grave is marked by a plain white wooden cross.

GLAMORGAN, WEST

OYSTERMOUTH

Thomas Bowdler (1754-1825), the surgeon and literary censor, published his very successful *Family Shakespeare* in 1818. It was an expurgated edition, giving rise to the verb 'to bowdlerise'. From 1810 until his death in 1825 he lived at Rhyddings, near Swansea. He was buried at All Saints' church, Oystermouth, near Bishopston, which is about 5 miles (8 km) south-west of Swansea; his grave is on the west side of the churchyard.

GWENT

LLANGATTOCK-VIBON-AVEL

The engineer and aviator **Charles Stewart Rolls** (1877-1910) was the third son of Baron Llangattock, whose home was The Hendre, near Monmouth. Charles Rolls pioneered the motor car in England, first setting up his own car-manufacturing business and then co-founding Rolls-Royce Ltd in 1904. He was killed at Bournemouth in a flying accident, thus becoming the first British victim of aviation. He was buried in the churchyard of St Cadoc's, at Llangattock-Vibon-Avel, near Monmouth; his grave is among those of the Llangattock family, a group of tall Celtic crosses.

TREDEGAR

The miner and Labour politician **Aneurin ('Nye') Bevan** (1897-1960) was educated in Tredegar, his family home. He married **Jennie Lee** (1904-88), who had become the Independent Labour Party MP for North Lanark at the age of twenty-four. As Minister of Health in the Attlee government, Nye Bevan was responsible for founding the National Health Service in 1946. He resigned from the cabinet in 1951, in protest at the introduction of prescription charges, but became deputy leader of the party in 1959. Bevan and Lee made their home at Asheridge Farm, near Chesham in Buckinghamshire; Bevan died there in 1960. He was cremated near Tredegar and his ashes were scattered in the Duffryn hills above his home town, as was his wish. Jennie Lee went on to become Minister for the Arts in Harold Wilson's Labour government and was responsible for establishing the Open University. After her death in 1988, she was cremated and her ashes were scattered at the same site as Bevan's had been, many years before.

GWYNEDD
LLANFIHANGEL-Y-TRAETHAU

The novelist, playwright and poet **Richard Arthur Warren Hughes** (1900-76) stayed on holiday near Talsarnau, a mile north-east of Llanfihangel-y-Traethau, when young; he lived near Talsarnau from 1947 until his death in 1976. His home was a house about a mile (just over a kilometre) north-west of Talsarnau, on the shore of the Dwyryd estuary opposite Portmeirion. He died at home and was buried in the churchyard of the church at Llanfihangel-y-Traethau on the Ynys, where he had been churchwarden.

LLANYSTUMDWY

The Liberal politician **David Lloyd George** (1863-1945), first Earl Lloyd-George of Dwyfor, prime minister 1916-22, was brought up at Llanystumdwy. He was buried on the bank of river Dwyfor, which flows through the village, and his grave was designed by the architect Clough Williams-Ellis, a friend and neighbour. In the centre of a simple oval enclosure bordering the river, entered through a wrought-iron gate, stands a huge boulder resting on cobblestones. Lloyd George's name and dates were inscribed on a pair of oval slate plaques by the sculptor Jonah Jones; these stand on the roadside, beside the gate. The area is now a World Heritage Site, but the grave has been altered by the addition of a rectangular slate plaque, hardly in keeping with the flowing lines of the enclosure.

RHOSCOLYN

The architect and town planner **Sir (Leslie) Patrick Abercrombie** (1879-1957), best known for his advocacy of regional planning after the Second World War, was buried at Rhoscolyn on Anglesey, in the setting of countryside he loved and had worked to preserve.

POWYS
CARNO

The dress designer, interior decorator and entrepreneur **Laura Ashley** (1925-85), born Laura Mountney at Dowlais near Merthyr Tydfil, married Bernard Albert Ashley in 1949. Laura Ashley eventually persuaded her husband to move to Wales, and they fell in love with mid-Wales whilst exploring the area. They moved to Machynlleth in 1963 and later settled at Carno, in the village's old railway station. Carno then became the headquarters of the vast international business of Laura Ashley plc. Laura Ashley, who died after a fall at her daughter's Cotswold home, was buried in the churchyard of St John the Baptist at Carno, just to the south of the Laura Ashley factory.

NEWTOWN

The socialist, industrialist and philanthropist **Robert Owen** (1771-1858) was born in Newtown and returned there to die. He was buried by the river in old St Mary's churchyard, outside the ruins of the south aisle of the old church, which was abandoned in the 1840s because of flooding. His monument, which dates from 1902, shows a relief of Owen and his workforce; the grave has superb Art Nouveau iron railings.

This bust of Jonathan Swift in St Patrick's Cathedral, Dublin, was carved in 1775 by Patrick Cunningham and was the gift of his publisher, T. T. Faulkner. Swift was Dean of the cathedral, and his pulpit stands in the north-west corner of the north transept. He was buried in the south aisle.

Ireland

CORK

CORK

The mathematician **George Boole** (1815-64), who developed Boolean algebra, was professor of mathematics at Queen's College, Cork, during 1849-64. He is buried in the churchyard of St Michael's, the Church of Ireland church at Blackrock, on the eastern edge of Cork.

The composer **Sir Arnold Edward Trevor Bax** (1883-1953) always had a special affinity for Irish poetry and countryside. He died in Cork and was buried in St Finbarr's Cemetery.

DURRUS

During the 1970s the novelist **James Gordon Farrell** (1935-79) lived near Kilcrohane, a small village on the north shore of Dunmanus Bay, 10 miles (16 km) south-west of Durrus. His small stone-built house overlooked Bantry Bay, where he drowned while fishing from a rock. He was buried at Durrus, in the churchyard of the Protestant church of St James, sited above Friendly Cove, Dunmanus Bay.

FARAHY
The family home of the novelist **Elizabeth Dorothea Cole Bowen** (1899-1973) was Bowen's Court, a little north-west of Farahy village and just under 2 miles (3 km) west of Kildorrery. Elizabeth Bowen was brought up there and inherited the house in 1928. She and her husband moved to Bowen's Court in 1952, but after his death the house proved too large and in 1960 it was sold; it has since been demolished. At her own wish, Elizabeth Bowen was buried in the churchyard of Kildorrey church, which lies within the grounds of Bowen's Court.

DUBLIN
DUBLIN
Jonathan Swift (1667-1745), the satirist who was Dean of St Patrick's Cathedral, Patrick Street, Dublin, during 1713-45, was buried beside his wife in the south aisle of St Patrick's.

Glasnevin Cemetery, Finglas Road, is Dublin's largest public cemetery; it tends to be associated with Catholics, as traditionally Protestants have preferred to use Mount Jerome Cemetery. At Glasnevin can be found the graves of several Irish heroes and political leaders, including **Charles Stewart Parnell** (1846-91), whose grave is topped by a granite boulder. Under a huge monument is the body of **Daniel O'Connell** (1775-1847), minus its heart, which at O'Connell's request was sent to Rome. Also here are the graves of **Michael Collins** (1890-1922), **Eamon De Valera** (1882-1975) and **Roger David Casement** (1864-1916), whose remains were returned to Ireland in 1965. Literary figures include the playwright **Brendan Behan** (1923-64) and the poet **Gerard Manley Hopkins** (1844-89). Hopkins was professor of classics at University College, Dublin. **Maude Gonne** (1865-1953), Irish revolutionary and the great but unrequited love of the poet W. B. Yeats is also here.

The dramatist **John Millington Synge** (1871-1909) was born and educated in Dublin. He spent his last years in or near the city and was buried at Mount Jerome Cemetery, Dublin's largest Protestant burial ground. Also buried here, in the Guinness family vault, was the Dublin brewer **Sir Benjamin Lee Guinness** (1798-1868), first baronet, who took over the family business from his father in 1855. He was Lord Mayor of Dublin in 1851 and restored St Patrick's Cathedral in 1860-5.

John Boyd Dunlop (1840-1921), the inventor and pioneer of the pneumatic rubber tyre, lived in Dublin for around thirty years and is buried in the cemetery at Deansgrange, a village near Dun Laoghaire.

GALWAY
GALWAY
William Brooke Joyce (1906-46), nicknamed 'Lord Haw-Haw' in reference to his voice on wartime propaganda broadcasts from Berlin, was buried in Bohermore Cemetery, Galway. He was born in the United States of America, the son of a builder from County Mayo, but the family lived in Ireland from 1909, before Joyce moved to England in 1921. He took out a British passport in 1933, falsely claiming his place of birth to be Galway. Joyce eventually founded the British National Socialist Party and left for Germany just before the start of the war. He was hanged at Wandsworth and his remains were moved to Galway in 1976.

KILDARE
BODENSTOWN
The republican hero **Theobald Wolfe Tone** (1763-98) led the United Irishmen's

Rising in 1798 and was captured by the British. He was condemned to death but committed suicide as he was refused a soldier's funeral. His grave is in the churchyard of the Church of Ireland church at Bodenstown.

SLIGO

DRUMCLIFF

As a boy, the poet and playwright **William Butler Yeats** (1865-1939) spent many holidays with his grandparents at Sligo and grew to love the countryside around the port town. Yeats died in the south of France, where he had gone to improve his health, and was given a temporary burial there. In 1948 his remains were brought back to Drumcliff, 4 miles (6 km) north of Sligo, as he had wished. He was finally buried in the graveyard of the Protestant church, where his grandfather was rector.

Some famous graves abroad

AUSTRALIA

ADELAIDE

The composer and pianist **(George) Percy Grainger** (1882-1961) was born in Australia; his parents were the English-born John Grainger and his wife Rose Aldridge, whose family had emigrated to Australia in 1847. Grainger, who is best known for his arrangements of English folksongs, studied in Melbourne and Frankfurt before touring extensively, finally making his home in the USA in 1915. Percy Grainger's final public performance was given in Hanover, New Hampshire, in April 1960; he died in America the following year, and his body was flown back to Australia. He had always been an atheist and requested that 'there be no public or religious funeral, funeral service or ceremony of any kind or nature'; however, his wishes were ignored. After an Anglican service at St Matthew's church, Marryatville, Adelaide, his body was placed in the Aldridge family vault at Adelaide's West Terrace Cemetery.

AUSTRIA

VIENNA

After the Second World War the poet **Wystan Hugh Auden** (1907-73) bought a house for use as a summer home at Kirchstetten, near Vienna. He died in Vienna and was buried at Kirchstetten.

CANADA

NEWCASTLE

The newspaper proprietor **William Maxwell Aitken** (1879-1964), first Baron Beaverbrook, was born in the township of Newcastle, New Brunswick, where he spent a happy childhood and attended the local school. He came to England in 1910 and bought his first newspaper, the *Daily Express*, in 1916. His ashes were buried in the town square in Newcastle; his bust stands on the plinth above them.

FRANCE

ANGERS

Margaret of Anjou (1430-82), queen consort of Henry VI, was brought up in Anjou and crowned queen in Westminster Abbey in 1445. After her husband was murdered in 1471 she was imprisoned but was eventually released, only to end her years in poverty in Anjou; she was buried at Angers.

AVIGNON

The political economist **John Stuart Mill** (1806-73) met the feminist **Harriet Taylor** (1807-58) in 1831 and married her in 1851, after the death of her husband. She died in France and was buried at Avignon, where Mill afterwards spent much of his time, dying there in 1873. He was buried in Avignon beside his wife.

CAEN

William the Conqueror (1027-87), king of England, was at war in Normandy when he died at Rouen after a riding accident. He was buried at St Stephen's church, Caen. A plain slab marks the site of the original grave, which was desecrated in 1793.

CHAMONIX

The alpinist **Edward Whymper** (1840-1911) made the first successful ascent of the Matterhorn (followed by a disastrous descent in which four of the party were killed) in 1865. He died in Chamonix, while on a visit to the Alps, and was buried in the churchyard of the English church at Chamonix.

FONTEVRAUD

The kings of England **Henry II** (1133-89) and **Richard I** (1157-99) both died in France and were buried at Fontevraud abbey church, although the heart of Richard Lionheart was buried at Rouen.

MENTON

The artist and illustrator **Aubrey Vincent Beardsley** (1872-98) was buried at Menton, where he died.

MULHOUSE

The designer and botanist **Christopher Dresser** (1834-1904) died at the Hotel Central, Mulhouse, and was buried at Mulhouse in an unmarked grave.

Henry II

PARIS

The dramatist and wit **Oscar O'Flahertie Wills Wilde** (1854-1900) spent his last years in France and died in Paris. He was buried at Bagneux Cemetery, on the outskirts of the city, but his remains were moved from Bagneux to Père Lachaise in 1909, and in 1914 a monument by Jacob Epstein (a massive Art Deco winged messenger) was placed at his grave. The monument bears an inscription from Wilde's *The Ballad of Reading Gaol* (1898). The writer, critic and arts administrator **Robert Baldwin Ross** (1869-1918), Wilde's literary executor and lifelong friend, was with Wilde when he died. Ross, a Roman Catholic, requested that after his own death his body should be cremated and the ashes be placed in Wilde's grave. He was indeed cremated in 1918, but the ashes were not taken to Paris to join Wilde until 30th November 1950, the fiftieth anniversary of Wilde's death.

The playwright **Samuel Beckett** (1906-89), who had made his home in France, was buried in the Cimitière du Montparnasse, just off Boulevard Raspail. He shares

Jacob Epstein's splendid monument to Oscar Wilde in the Père Lachaise cemetery, Paris. The monument was three years in the making and after its installation in 1914 was deemed to be indecent by the cemetery authorities. A plaque was eventually placed over the unacceptable part of the winged messenger's anatomy, and the problem was soon permanently solved by the actions of students, who hacked away lumps of stone as souvenirs.

the grave with his wife Suzanne Deschevaux-Dumesnil, who had died a few months earlier; they had been together for over fifty years.

ROUEN
The king of England **Richard I** (1157-99) died in France and was buried at Fontevraud abbey church, although his heart was buried at Rouen. **John of Lancaster** (1389-1435), Duke of Bedford, and third son of Henry IV, died at Rouen and was also buried there.

ST CLOUD
The actress **Dorothea Jordan** (1762-1816), long-term mistress of the Duke of Clarence (later William IV), went to France in 1815 and died at St Cloud, where she was buried.

ST DENIS
Henrietta Maria (1609-69), queen consort of Charles I, died at St Colombes and was buried at St Denis.

ST GERMAIN
James II (1633-1701), king of England, died at the palace of St Germain, near Paris, and was buried there; the remains were rediscovered and re-interred at St Germain in 1824.

GERMANY
HANOVER
George I (1660-1727), king of Great Britain and Ireland, died of apoplexy at Osnabrück and was buried in the vaults of his palace at Hanover.

GREECE
SCYROS
The poet **Rupert Chawner Brooke** (1887-1915) died of blood poisoning whilst at sea off the Greek island of Scyros on his way to the Dardanelles. He was buried in the corner of an olive grove on Scyros.

ITALY
FLORENCE
The poet **Walter Savage Landor** (1775-1864) died in Florence and was buried in the English cemetery in Piazza Donatello.

LIVORNO
The novelist **Tobias George Smollett** (1721-71), who had lived in Italy from time to time from 1763, died at his home at Monte Nero, near Livorno, and was buried in the English cemetery.

ROME
James Francis Edward Stewart (1688-1766), Prince of Wales and 'Old Pretender', settled in Rome in 1719 and was buried at St Peter's. His sons **Charles Edward Stewart, 'Bonnie Prince Charlie'** (1720-88), and **Cardinal Henry Stewart** (1725-1807) are also there. The monument over their tomb was erected in 1819 by George III and designed by Canova.

The poet **Percy Bysshe Shelley** (1792-1822) left England for Italy in 1819. In 1822 he set sail from Livorno in his small schooner and was lost in a storm. His body was recovered and cremated on a beach; the ashes, minus his heart, which was snatched from the flames, were buried in the Protestant cemetery in Rome. His heart now shares the grave of his wife, Mary Wollstonecraft Shelley (1797-1851) in the

The grave of the poet John Keats and his friend, the artist Joseph Severn (1799-1879), in the Protestant cemetery, Rome. Keats had come to Rome hoping to recover from tuberculosis but died a few months later, attended by Severn, who eventually became the British consul in Rome. On Keats's tomb is the epitaph which he composed himself: 'Here lies one whose name was writ in water.'

churchyard of St Peter, Hinton Road, Bournemouth. The author and adventurer **Edward John Trelawny** (1792-1881) met Percy Shelley in Italy in 1821 and was at Livorno when Shelley drowned. He was buried by Shelley's side in the Protestant cemetery. In the same cemetery is the grave of the poet **John Keats** (1795-1821). Keats sailed for Italy in September 1820, reaching Rome in November; he died there in February 1821.

The portrait painter **Angelica Kauffman** (1741-1807) studied in Florence and Rome before coming to England; she returned to Rome permanently in 1781. She died and was buried in Rome at Sant Andrea delle Fratte.

SAN REMO

The artist and author **Edward Lear** (1812-88), who published *A Book of Nonsense* in 1845, settled in San Remo in 1871. He spent the rest of his life there and was buried in San Remo.

JAMAICA

The actor, composer and producer **Sir Noël Pierce Coward** (1899-1973) visited Jamaica in 1948 and fell in love with the island. He built a house, Blue Harbour, on its coast and in 1956 put up a small retreat called Firefly Hill on the hillside above. He died at Firefly Hill, where he was buried. His grave, marked by a plain white marble slab, overlooks the view he had loved.

KENYA

NYERI

Robert Stephenson Smyth Baden-Powell (1857-1941), first Baron Baden-Powell, founded the Boy Scouts in 1907. His wife, **Lady Olave St Clair Baden-Powell** (1889-1977), was prominent within the Girl Guides and became the World Chief Guide in 1932. The Baden-Powells spent two weeks at Nyeri in 1935, on their way to South Africa. Lord Baden-Powell found Nyeri a magical place, and they eventually settled there, in a bungalow named Paxtu, in 1938. Lord Baden-Powell died at Paxtu and was buried in the cemetery at Nyeri. Lady Olave Baden-Powell died at Guildford; her ashes were flown to Kenya and buried in her husband's grave.

NORWAY

OSLO

George Bradshaw (1801-53) was an engraver and printer who worked at first in Belfast and then in Manchester. In 1839 he produced the *Railway Time Tables*, which developed into *Bradshaw's Monthly Railway Guides*, first published in 1841. In August 1853 Bradshaw went on a tour to Norway, combining business and pleasure. While visiting a friend near Oslo, he began to show symptoms of cholera and died within a few hours. He was buried in a cemetery belonging to Oslo Cathedral.

PANAMA

PORTOBELO

The circumnavigator and admiral **Sir Francis Drake** (1540?-96) died at sea off Portobelo, on the north coast of Panama, and was buried at sea in a lead coffin. There are plans to locate the coffin and return it to England.

SAMOA

The author and traveller **Robert Louis Stevenson** (1850-94), formerly Robert Lewis Balfour Stevenson, set out for the south seas in 1888. He finally settled at Vailima on Samoa in 1890. He died on Samoa and was buried there at a spot he selected on Mount Vaea.

Robert Louis Stevenson.

SPAIN
DEYA (MAJORCA)
The writer and poet **Robert Ranke Graves** (1895-1985) lived in Majorca during 1929-36 and returned to live on the island permanently in 1946. His home was on the outskirts of Deya, a hill village near the north coast, where he built a house called Caín Alluny. Graves produced some of his finest work at Deya. He is buried under a simple concrete slab in the churchyard above the village; the inscription 'R Graves, Poeta' was written into the drying concrete at the funeral. Cyprus trees shade the grave.

SWITZERLAND
CHÂTEAU D'OEX
The actor **(James) David (Graham) Niven** (1910-83) spent many of his later years skiing at Château d'Oex; he died at his home there and was buried in the village.

CORSEAUX
The novelist **(Henry) Graham Greene** (1904-91) died in Vevey, Switzerland. He was buried in the churchyard of St Jean in the hamlet of Corseaux, overlooking Lake Geneva from the slopes of Mount Pelerin.

GENEVA
The scientist **Sir Humphry Davy** (1778-1829), inventor of the safety lamp, went to Italy to improve his health in 1827. By March 1828 he was in Rome; he left for Geneva but died the day after his arrival there and was buried in the cemetery of Plain-Palais.

UNITED STATES
CALIFORNIA
The ashes of the writer **Jessica Lucy Mitford** (1917-96) were scattered in the sea off San Francisco, California. She had settled at Oakland with her second husband after the Second World War and published her exposé of the funeral business, *The American Way of Death*, in 1963; she was working on a new edition of the book when she died. As befitted that of a campaigner against overcharging and malpractice in the funeral trade, her own funeral (which involved a cremation with no ceremony), arranged by the Pacific Interment Service, cost a mere $533.31, or about £320.

ZIMBABWE
MATAPO
Cecil John Rhodes (1858-1902), the imperialist and founder of Rhodesia, now Zimbabwe, was buried at View of the World in the Matapo Hills, now a national park.

Further reading

Bailey, B. *Churchyards of England and Wales*. Robert Hale, 1987.
Black, J. *The Glasgow Graveyard Guide*. Saint Andrew Press, 1992.
Brooks, C. *Burying Tom Sayers: Heroism, Class and the Victorian Cemetery*. Victorian Society Annual, 1989.
Brooks, C. *Mortal Remains*. Wheaton, 1989.
Colvin, H. *Architecture and the After-life*. Yale University Press, 1991.
Culbertson, J., and Randall, T. *Permanent Londoners*. Robson Books, 1991.
Culbertson, J., and Randall, T. *Permanent Parisians*. Chelsea Green, 1986.
Curl, J. S. *A Celebration of Death*. Constable, 1980.
Eagle, D., and Stephens, M. (editors). *The Oxford Literary Guide to Great Britain and Ireland*. Oxford University Press, 1993.
Greenwood, D. *Who's Buried Where in England*. Constable, 1990.
Kerrigan, M. *Who Lies Where*. Fourth Estate, 1995.
Lee, J. *Who's Buried Where in Leicestershire*. Leicestershire Libraries and Information Service, 1991.
Lees, H. *Hallowed Ground*. Thornhill Press, 1993.
Love, D. *Scottish Kirkyards*. Robert Hale, 1989.
McKenna, J. *In the Midst of Life*. Birmingham Library Services, 1992.
Meller, H. *London Cemeteries*. Scolar Press, 1994.
Murray, H. *The York Graveyard Guide*. Saint Andrew Press, 1994.
Murray, H. *This Garden of Death*. Friends of York Cemetery, 1988.
Turnbull, M. R. T. B. *The Edinburgh Graveyard Guide*. Saint Andrew Press, 1991.
Westminster Abbey. Dean and Chapter of Westminster, 1997.

Also consulted were many guides to individual churchyards, cemeteries and burial grounds, and many biographies and biographical guides, most importantly the *Dictionary of National Biography*.

Societies

BIRKENHEAD
Friends of Flaybrick. John Moffat, 76 St John's Road, Eastham, Wirral L62 0BW. Telephone: 0151-327 7528.

BRISTOL
Association for the Preservation of Arnos Vale Cemetery. Richard Smith, 15 Aintree Drive, Downend, Bristol BS16 6SY. Telephone: 0117-957 3066.

BROOKWOOD
The Brookwood Cemetery Society. Barbara Farish, 37 Victoria Road, Knaphill, Woking, Surrey GU21 2AH. Telephone: 01483 472086. Regular guided walks, lectures and newsletters, and a wide range of publications. Annual open day.

EDINBURGH
Edinburgh Cemeteries Support Group. Ann Combe, 13/3 Sleigh Gardens, Edinburgh EH7 6EL.
Morningside Association. Irene Burnie, 11 Dalhousie Terrace, Edinburgh EH10 5NE.

LEEDS
Friends of Beckett Street Cemetery. Sylvia Barnard, 2 North Park Road, Leeds, West Yorkshire LS8 1JD. Telephone: 0113-266 7456.

LONDON
Friends of Abney Park Cemetery. c/o Abney Park Cemetery Trust, South Lodge, Abney Park Cemetery, Stoke Newington High Street, London N16 0LN. Telephone: 0171-275 7557. Guided walks, lectures, newsletters, publications.
Friends of Brompton Cemetery. Emma Arbuthnot, 58 Ifield Road, London SW10. Telephone: 0171-352 3974.
Friends of Hampstead Cemetery. Dr Marianne Colloms, 69 Fortune Green Road, London NW6 1DR.
Friends of Highgate Cemetery. Highgate Cemetery, Swains Lane, London N6 6PJ. Telephone: 0181-340 1834.
Friends of Kensal Green Cemetery. Henry Vivian-Neal, 17 Buchanan Gardens, London NW10 5AD. Telephone: 0181-960 1030. Guided walks, catacomb tours, lectures, a wide range of publications and newsletters. Annual open day.
Friends of Nunhead Cemetery. Ron Woolacott, 185 Gordon Road, London SE15 3RT. Telephone: 0171-732 2501. Guided walks, talks, publications and newsletters. Annual open day.
Friends of Tottenham Cemetery. Ashley Grey, 1 Prospect Place, Church Lane, London N17 8AT.
Friends of Tower Hamlets Cemetery Park. Stewart Rayment, 1 Lockhart Street, London E3 4BL. Telephone: 0181-983 0504. Nature walks.
Friends of West Norwood Cemetery. Jill Dudman, 119 Broxholm Road, London SE27 0BJ. Telephone: 0181-670 5456. Guided walks, lectures, newsletters and publications.
Friends of Woodgrange Park Cemetery. Mrs D. Bedford, 66 Hillview Avenue, Hornchurch, Essex RM22 2DW.

NORWICH
Friends of the Rosary Cemetery. Mrs B Nierop-Reading, 4 Bathurst Road, Norwich, Norfolk NR2 2PP. Telephone: 01603 623697.

SHEFFIELD
Friends of the General Cemetery. Jane Horton, 223 Cemetery Road, Sheffield, South Yorkshire S11 8FQ. Telephone: 0114-255 6092.

SHEPTON MALLET
Friends of Shepton Mallet Cemetery. Irene Venner, 2 Stevens Close, Ridgeway, Shepton Mallet, Somerset. Telephone: 01749 343249.

YORK
Friends of York Cemetery. Barbara Durack, 43 St John Street, York YO3 7QR. Telephone: 01904 647202. Guided walks, newsletters and publications. Nature garden.

OTHER USEFUL ADDRESSES
The Living Churchyard and Cemetery Project. David Manning, Arthur Rank Centre, National Agricultural Centre, Stoneleigh Park, Warwickshire CV8 2LZ. Telephone: 01203 696969.
Memorials by Artists. Harriet Frazer, Snape Priory, Saxmundham, Suffolk IP17 1SA. Telephone: 01728 688934. Produces original hand-carved memorials. Booklet available.
National Association of Memorial Masons. Teresa Quinn, Crown Buildings, High Street, Aylesbury, Buckinghamshire HP20 1SL. Telephone: 01296 434750. Trade association for memorial masons.
National Federation of Cemetery Friends. Gwyneth Stokes, 42 Chestnut Grove, South Croydon, Surrey CR2 7LH. Telephone: 0181-651 5090.

Index of persons